NUCLEAR HEARTLAND

A guide to the 1,000
missile silos of the United States

A Nukewatch book

Edited by Samuel H. Day, Jr.

Photo portraits by John Hooton

Foreword by Philip Berrigan

The Progressive Foundation
315 West Gorham Street
Madison, Wisconsin 53703

NUCLEAR HEARTLAND

THE PROGRESSIVE FOUNDATION, INC.
315 West Gorham Street
Madison, Wisconsin 53703

Library of Congress Catalog Card Number: 88-61904

ISBN: 0-942046-01-3

Cover photo © by John Hooton

Book design: Bonnie Urfer

Printed in the U.S.A.
by Community Publications, Inc.
McFarland, Wisconsin

Contents

Foreword 4

Introduction 6

I: The Buildup 8

II: The Awakening 19

III: Missile Silos of the United States
          Wyoming, Nebraska, and Colorado 27
          North Dakota
                    Minot AFB 37
                    Grand Forks AFB 45
          South Dakota.....................................52
          Montana 60
          Missouri 71

IV: In Missile Silo Country 79

V: Beacons of Hope 92

Postscript..96

4

Foreword

by Philip Berrigan

ABOUT 1966, U THANT, then Secretary General of the United Nations, remarked that if the American people knew the truth about the Indochina War they would stop it.

In the fall of 1987, while on trial for attempting to block the Maryland National Guard from flying south to Honduras, I cross-examined an Air Force security officer testifying against us: "Captain, are you aware that nuclear weapons have made war and the military obsolete?" The judge allowed him to answer, and he said, "No!"

Clearly, the government took strenuous measures to prevent Americans from learning the truth about the Indochina war, just as today it extends itself even further to prevent military personnel and all of us from knowing the truth about nuclear insanity. Truth and war are inimical—no war-making government can tolerate the luxury of an informed and critical public.

I do not claim that anyone knows the whole truth about the nuclear curse, in all its depraved and tragic aspects. Given that, however, what does one need to know? If these weapons are not immoral, evil, unjust, and anti-human, then nothing is. And we had better kiss the human experiment goodbye, for there's no way to salvage it.

I do claim, nonetheless, that any knowledge of it is underknowledge, and any statement describing it is understatement. Many know it historically, or biologically, or technically, but do not know it morally. And all fail in describing its horror.

But we must try. Sidney Lens tried until his death, at one point writing that the nuclear madness was a greater disaster than all previous natural or human catastrophes. Even of the sum of them. Understatement, it seems to me.

Others have asserted that 43 years of historical distortion and Red Scares by American elites to install a permanent war economy and to legitimize nuclear terror eclipse the demagoguery and savagery of Hitler and Stalin, with more profound and widespread consequences. Again, understatement.

Others will point to the shameless and miserable failure of world institutions—governments, churches, media, campuses (especially Western institutions)—to expose nuclear lunacy and to propose human alternatives. Once more, understatement.

Let the reader please understand that this foreword is not overclaim but understatement; that the book itself is understatement; that anything that anyone can say or write about the degeneracy of nuclear idolatry would be understatement.

But we must try to state the unstateable, to comprehend the incomprehensible. It is only after looking into the pit of this nuclear hell that we can see beyond to a world without war.

We must try to grasp three minutes to nuclear midnight. Or our children caught in the Anne Frank syndrome, without a future.

We must sorrow over our rape of God's creation—our poisoning of it and our plans to destroy it.

We must comprehend the hostageship of five billion of us, on a *real* nuclear death row.

We must ponder the reality of 150 million tons of radioactive garbage in the stratosphere from testing—over one-half of it American—sifting into the air, water and soil. Let ecologists take note.

We must scrutinize our willingness to pay for these hellish weapons with the death of 40,000 children daily.

We must fathom the colossal, unparalleled and savage injustice of nuclearism. And take responsibility for it. If we don't, our injustice will become terminal, and we will die of it.

We must, in other words, imagine the unimaginable, think the unthinkable, describe the indescribable and do the impossible.

One way to understand the Bomb is to reckon what it has cost us spiritually. It has, among other things, redefined slavery. Americans are the first people in history to pay for the prospect of their own destruction, while calling it the price of freedom. Meanwhile, we have had available to us every constitutional guarantee for protest and dissent. Our people have not only paid for the weapons, but have built them and deployed them, contributing in the process their young people and silence to the deadly agenda.

The realities of this abject bondage are neither understood nor admitted. Rather, they are diverted into fantasies of freedom. In this matter, the yardstick of comparison is the Russians, never the Germans, never the Nazis.

We have here new connotations of slavery, with the accent on moral slavery, like the Bible's understanding of the term. Because most Americans have never taken responsibility for Hiroshima and Nagasaki; have never renounced complicity in the leadership of the arms race; have never ceased being a cog in the infernal war machine of the pharaohs, we have become, unconsciously for the most part, the most total and pitiful of slaves. Meanwhile, we ape the politicians, congratulating one another on our freedom.

Another way to comprehend the Bomb is to mull over its economic cost. (I use Bomb generically, as a metaphor for war preparations and war. Indeed, it is dominant in any phase of military policy; it dictates to those who possess it.)

Since 1946, the U.S. has spent about five trillion dollars on past, present and future wars. This deranged sum equals or slightly surpasses that spent by humankind on war in the same period. But we are 6 per cent of the world's people.

Without breaking down this obscene outlay into domestic or "diplomatic" components, its bottom line is simply this—insurance for our "right" to consume over one-third of what the world produces as one-sixteenth of its people. Yes, six or seven times our rightful share.

The main check on this criminal extravagance has not been dissent or resistance alone, but rather the bankruptcy of the empire, and its humiliating decline from creditor to debtor status.

A final way to measure the Bomb is to assess its political cost. For example, how many governments do Americans have? The elected one, the commercial and financial one, the gumshoe one, the Secret Team one. Some say three; some say four.

Whatever the case, government amounts to fundamentalism of the Right, an elitist fascism that propagandizes a democracy which no longer exists. What we know as government no longer represents the people: Their votes merely signal a change in the palace guard, responsible like the last mediocrities in power to the hidden governments. As for the people, they get ruling rather than governing, plus distractions of bread and circuses, in the old imperial model.

The Bomb, of course, is the imperial fundamental—it is the showcase American idol. And idols are always totalitarian. When people make the Faustian bargain with them, the terms of contract are absolute. Watch the Pharaohs choose between their people and the Bomb. They will choose the Bomb; in fact, they have

done so already.

Nukewatch and this book are essentially two things: a reminder and a human alternative. A reminder against imperial amnesia; a human alternative against deadly, paralyzing fear. Amnesia and fear are more potent destroyers than the Bomb.

The Nukewatch people—Sam Day, Barb Katt, John LaForge and other friends—won't let us alone. They won't allow us to put our heads up our rectums, or slink behind the woodwork, or to take a job in a war plant. The missiles are here and here and there, they say. Come and see that 120-ton cover, or a crew changing a warhead, or experience a 19-year-old tracking you with a machine gun because you leaned on the fence. And meditate on what's in that hole, and what will happen if young launch officers trip those keys.

Said one launch officer some years ago at Whiteman Air Force Base in Missouri: "If we fire these missiles, I won't be taking the elevator to the surface. There won't be anything there!"

Furthermore, the Nukewatch people do more than map the silos, or travel 30,000 miles to do it. They break the anti-laws which legalize these monsters. They put flesh on their words, and by doing that say to us: We don't have to take betrayal and slavery and poison and hostageship to the Bomb. We can raise our voices and use our hands and invest our bodies in a huge, resounding, unequivocal public NO!—and a sacred YES! to life.

It's a question of what we believe, they say. If we don't believe in the God of the Bible, the God of compassion and justice (some of us try), then believe in people like Helen Woodson, Jean Gump, Carl Kabat, Larry Morlan, Jerry Ebner, Joe Gump and other Plowshares who have disarmed these hammers of hell. They're the remnant that has come out of slavery. They're the new woman, the new man. They're the handle on the future.

The Nukewatch people say, C'mon, join them. Join us. All we'll lose is our ball and chain.

Editor's postscript: This foreword was written in the Rappahanock Security Center at Fredericksburg, Virginia, where the author awaited sentencing for disarming two Tomahawk cruise missile launchers on board the USS Iowa at the Norfolk Naval Base on April 3, 1988 (Easter Sunday). He acted with Sister Margaret McKenna of Philadelphia and with Greg Boertje and Andrew Lawrence, fellow residents of Jonah House in Baltimore.

6

Introduction

Jeannie Bernstein

Unseen victims, unseen weapons.

THE SOIL OF THE North American Great Plains is seeded with a thousand intercontinental ballistic missiles—sentinels of the nuclear age—each built to be launched on 31 seconds' notice. This book is about that unseen underground weapon system—how it got there, what it looks like, how it works, how it has affected the people who live close to it, and how you can find it for yourself. But the story begins, appropriately, in a school room in Soviet Russia.

Leafing one day through a friend's snapshots from a tour of the Soviet Union, I stopped at a scene of children in a Moscow elementary school. They made a pretty picture, standing there in their school uniforms, hair neatly combed, faces scrubbed, eyes gleaming. But what riveted my attention was not so much the children as a large map on the wall behind them. The map showed the familiar outlines of the United States. The heads and shoulders of the students framed the midsection of the country. You could trace the thick blue line of the Missouri River, draining the Great Plains and upper Midwest from the Rockies to the Ozarks.

Unknowingly, the Moscow school children, anxious to make a good impression on a visitor from the United States, had framed with their bodies an area of the country comprising the very region from which nuclear warheads may one day rain down on them. As residents of a prime target city, their fate was programmed into computers aboard intercontinental ballistic missiles poised for firing from within the vastness caught by the camera's eye. By purest chance, they had formed the perfect juxtaposition of potential victim and potential assailant. They were as oblivious of that irony as were my friend and the other American visitors smiling back at them across the classroom.

The photograph of the Moscow school children found a place in a series of missile silo maps produced by Nukewatch over the next two years—together with photos showing the visible parts of U.S. intercontinental ballistic missile launch sites and launch control centers. The purpose of the photographs was to call attention to the unseen victims and the unseen weapons, cradled in underground tubes shaped like the silos that store the harvest of an abundant agricultural region.

The existence of long-range nuclear missiles based in the United States and the Soviet Union and aimed at each other's heartland is common knowledge. But for most people it is a knowledge grown abstract, imprecise, and devoid of feeling. The underground missile systems of the two superpowers, each capable of causing unimaginable death and destruction, are out of sight and out of mind. Few Americans can pick out a missile launch site from the many that stand within easy sight of heavily traveled interstate highways and winding country roads. The innocuous looking outcroppings in fields and prairies have become virtually invisible even to many residents of missile silo country.

The purpose of the missile mapping project, conducted by volunteers in the missile states, was to raise public awareness of the unseen weapons, to strip them

6

of their anonymity, to demystify them, to make them more accessible to the public, and to encourage people to approach them and contemplate their meaning. This was undertaken in the knowledge that being just a few yards from a nuclear warhead can provide a psychological spur—a stimulus to greater action against participation in the nuclear arms race. That is also the purpose of this book—a compilation of the six regional missile silo maps.

Nuclear Heartland is the work of many people. They include, most notably, Bonnie Urfer, who produced the finished maps, and other Nukewatch staff members Bert Zipperer, Laurie Frank, and Jane Simonds; missile silo activists Susan B. Nelson, Lilias Jones, Larry and Lindy Lange, and Kristin Sorenson, who provided much inspiration and help; regional mapping coordinators Roy Pell in Missouri, Mary Clark-Kaiser in North Dakota, Lorraine and Peter Holcomb in Wyoming, Mark Anderlik in Montana, and Mike Sprong and Beth Preheim in South Dakota, and production assistants Bill Stafford, Ericka Overgard, and Maurice Thaler. Special thanks, also, to Barb Katt and John LaForge, who drove 30,000 miles to recheck the map locations of all 1,000 missile silos and 100 launch control centers.

The Progressive Foundation, Inc., of which Nukewatch is the educational arm, also gratefully acknowledges the contributions of Carol and Ping Ferry of Scarsdale, New York; the Otto Bremer Foundation, St. Paul, Minnesota; the Samuel Rubin Foundation, the New Land Foundation, and Ann R. Roberts, all of New York, New York, The Sisters of Loretto, Denver, Colorado, the CS Fund of Freestone, California, and many other Nukewatch supporters whose financial help made the book possible.

Samuel H. Day, Jr., editor
Nukewatch
Madison, Wisconsin
September, 1988

Cover photo: The Rockies, looking west from missile silo F8, near Clemons Coulee, Montana.

© John Hooton

THE PHOTOGRAPHER

The missile silo photo portraits on the cover of this book and on Pages 27, 37, 52, 60, 71, and 95 were made for Nukewatch by John Hooton of Bozeman, Montana, associate professor of photography at Montana State University. While on assignment he paused at silo I6, near Cascade, Montana, for this family self-portrait with daughters Reagan and Alicia.

THE EDITOR

Samuel H. Day, Jr., co-director of Nukewatch, was editor of *The Bulletin of the Atomic Scientists* and managing editor of *The Progressive* before joining Nukewatch in 1981. He is the author of many articles on nuclear weapons issues.

NUKEWATCH

The educational arm of The Progressive Foundation, a nonprofit public interest group based in Madison, Wisconsin, Nukewatch endeavors to raise public awareness of nuclear weapons in the United States. In addition to mapping nuclear missile silos, Nukewatch tracks highway shipments of nuclear warheads and produces citizen's action guides to nuclear weapons laboratories, factories, and storage depots.

Chapter I:
The Buildup

A BUSY FARMER, Donald Lee of Devils Lake, North Dakota, paid little attention to the missile silo the Air Force installed in his wheat field in 1966. Sunk into the ground, covered by a concrete lid, enclosed by a fence with barbed wire on top, the missile occupied a world of its own at the end of a gravel road just off the highway. He drove past it almost daily.

Then one day the Air Force took the missile out of its hole and hauled it away for repairs.

"It's a huge thing," farmer Lee told a visiting reporter from Winnipeg. "I never dreamt how deep that hole is. I've often thought about what would happen if I was on my tractor near the silo and that missile took off. I didn't realize it had so much destructive power."

Most people who have intercontinental ballistic missiles as neighbors don't get to see what's in the hole. Some have left their farms in the quarter century since the silos were dug and then covered up. For the rest, the Air Force has been careful to keep the missiles covered and onlookers at a distance when maintenance work was under way behind the silo fence.

Most farmers like Donald Lee become fatalistic, even nonchalant, about living at Ground Zero. "After you've walked around a barrel of dynamite for 20 years, and it doesn't hurt you, you sort of don't think about it," says Tony Ziden, who farms at Pisek, North Dakota.

Fatalism also is the rule in other parts of the United States where the front line of the nuclear arms race runs through the back forty. Only a few yards below ground, often just a short drive from schools, churches, and shopping centers, these fine-tuned rockets with nuclear payloads are part of the landscape, as familiar as fence posts and telephone poles. "Most of these missile silos are on country roads," says Dr. Al Aldrich, a retired physician who lives not far from several of them in the pastoral ranch land of southeastern Wyoming. "They look like someone started to build a house and ran out of money, covered it over with a ce-

Minuteman missile test launch: More destructive than all the bombs dropped on the Soviet Union in World War II.

ment slab, and put a fence around it."

From nearby public roads, the launch sites are inconspicuous. Occupying only a couple of acres each, they exhibit little more than a few poles and metal parts around a large, flat, concrete slab—the missile silo lid. They could be easily mistaken for small electrical power substations. The crews who operate, maintain, and guard the launch facilities work in farm-like buildings atop blast-proof concrete bunkers deep underground. They travel to and from their posts in Air Force vans, as unconnected to the world outside their windows—and as unnoticed by it—as office workers headed for town on an early morning commuter train.

What Donald Lee saw coming out of the hole in his wheat field was a 39-ton Minuteman III intercontinental ballistic missile, taller (at 59 feet, 11 inches) than any office building in Devils Lake. Assembled in a factory hundreds of miles away from parts manufactured all over the United States, it had been flown to an air force base ninety miles from his home and transported to his farm in an air-conditioned tractor-trailer designed to cushion it against the slightest jolt. Fitted with two or three nuclear warheads each 15 to 25 times more powerful than the atomic bomb that destroyed Hiroshima in 1945, the missile was capable of reaching any target in the Soviet Union.

The missile had four sets of three targets each programmed into its computers. With the appropriate target selection, it could cause more death and destruction than all the bombs dropped on the Soviet Union by Nazi Germany in World War II.

The command to launch would come by underground cable from a bunker buried in another field seven miles away, near the town of Hampden. Above ground, the command post presented an unimposing one-story structure with a basketball hoop and backboard outside. But in the capsule below, two Air Force officers (a captain and a lieutenant, probably both in their 20s) controlled the firing mechanism for the Donald Lee missile and nine others spread across several hundred square miles of farmland between Devils Lake and Canada. Computers in the control center could order 100 different target combinations, giving the ten missiles the capability of crippling the Soviet Union.

On computer screens at the U.S. Air Force Strategic Air Command (SAC) headquarters at Offutt Air Force Base near Omaha, Nebraska, the missile in Donald Lee's wheat field is one of a thousand dots on a grid covering half the length of the United States. It is designated E46—a symbol also displayed on a large metal plate on the silo fence. E46 (or "Echo 46" in Air Force parlance) is one of ten missiles in E Flight, controlled by "Echo Zero," the command post near Hampden, North Dakota.

Five flights make up a missile squadron. Three squadrons comprise a wing—the 321st Strategic Missile Wing, headquartered at Grand Forks Air Force Base near Grand Forks, North Dakota. The fifteen flights and 150 missiles controlled by the 321st stretch from Interstate Highway 94 north to the Canadian border, an area roughly the size and shape of the state of New Jersey.

Grand Forks Air Force Base and Minot Air Force Base, 200 miles to the west, with equivalent missile strength, together make North Dakota the world's third-ranked nuclear weapons power—after the United States and the Soviet Union. The 300 nuclear missiles of the "Peace Garden State," farmed by the descendants of sturdy German and Scandinavian immigrants, are down the road from towns named Munich, Dresden, Karlsruhe, Kongsberg, and Berthold. With other missile silo fields to the west and south, they comprise the land-based intercontinental missile force of the United States. In addition to the missiles of North Dakota, four other fields of destruc-

tion cast a shadow over the Great Plains.

To the west, centered at Malmstrom Air Force Base at Great Falls, Montana, a field of 200 missile silos and 20 launch control centers covers 12 per cent of the land mass of the nation's fourth largest state. Roads to the launch sites of Montana lie across paths followed by explorers Meriwether Lewis and William Clark in 1805 to open the Pacific Northwest to white trade and settlement, and by the U.S. cavalry 72 years later, pursuing the exhausted army of Chief Joseph of the Nez Perces, to close the same country to the free movement of its original inhabitants.

In South Dakota, a field of 150 missiles abuts the Black Hills, sacred to the Indians of that region. In the High Plains where Wyoming, Colorado, and Nebraska come together, missile silos parallel the old Oregon Trail as it begins its slow climb out of the Platte River valley toward the Rockies. The sixth missile field is in Missouri, the "Show Me" state, where silos are tucked away off country roads leading out of Cole Camp, Tightwad, and Booneville, near the Schell-Osage Wildlife Area and the Harry S. Truman Reservoir, and close by Confederate Memorial State Park near the town of Higginsville.

The U.S. force of 1,000 land-based missiles with 2,310 warheads is smaller than that of the Soviet Union (with 6,856 warheads on 1,400 land-based missiles). But with U.S. superiority in submarine-launched missiles and long-range bombers, the two superpowers have more than enough strategic nuclear capability for mutually assured destruction.

The missile silos of the U.S. Strategic Air Command, located in Missouri, North and South Dakota, Montana, and the three adjacent corners of Wyoming, Nebraska, and Colorado—the "Minuteman" silos—are what's left of several generations of land-based ICBMs that have come and gone in seventeen states since 1958. They are a small part of the strategic (long range) nuclear weaponry maintained by the U.S. armed forces—other warheads are launched from Navy submarines or dropped from Air Force bombers. The underground launch sites in the Great Plains are an even smaller part of the Pentagon's entire nuclear arsenal, consisting of some 25,000 bombs and warheads fitted into artillery shells, land mines, and missiles of many kinds. But they are unique in one respect. Unlike other nuclear armaments of the United States and other military powers, Minuteman missiles are interwoven with the lives of the people in whose midst they have been placed. There's nothing secret

Atlas, 1959-1968

Maps on these two pages show deployment of four generations of intercontinental ballistic missiles. Above, Atlas missiles were based from 1959 to 1968 at Omaha and Lincoln, NE; Cheyenne, WY; Spokane, WA; Topeka and Salina, KS; Altus, OK; Abilene, TX; Roswell, NM; Lompoc, CA, and Plattsburgh, NY.

Titan, 1962-1987

The Titan missile generation was from 1962 to 1987. Titan I was based at Denver, CO; Marysville, CA; Moses Lake, WA; Mountain Home, ID, and Rapid City, SD. Titan II was based at Tucson, AZ; Wichita, KS, and Little Rock, AR.

MX, 1986-

Deployment of the MX (Peacekeeper) mobile missile system started in 1986 when the first of the ten-warhead missiles were installed in Minuteman silos in southeastern Wyoming. Air Force plans call for deployment of additional MX missiles on rail cars stationed at Cheyenne and various other bases in the western United States.

about where the silos are or what's in them. Albeit protected by impenetrable steel and concrete and by armed Air Force guards only a short drive away, the unattended missile silos are uniquely approachable and accessible. At a time when nuclear weapons and nuclear war itself are retreating ever farther from public visibility and public consciousness, the thousand launch sites of the Great Plains are available for seeing and for contemplating. They offer a tangible link with the reality of the global nuclear threat. Potentially, they are needles capable of pricking a public long numbed to the nuclear danger.

One of the realities that has yet to sink in on the residents of missile silo country—conservative, patriotic, trusting people, mostly—is that their part of the United States was chosen long ago by distant strategists to serve as a national sacrifice area. The strategy is evident in the pattern of the missile silos around Donald Lee's farm.

Starting from a point north of the farm, the ten launch sites of Flight E in the Grand Forks missile silo field form a rough circle around launch control center Echo Zero, like a rim around the hub of a wheel. That pattern is generally true of all Minuteman missile flights, varying somewhat with the terrain. Each missile silo is supposed to be at least 4.2 miles from the next one. There's a reason for that, seldom mentioned by the Air Force in its dealings with local farmers and townspeople.

Early planners of the Minuteman basing system wanted the silos far enough apart so that no two could be knocked out by the same incoming warhead. They designed a protective sheath of steel and concrete capable of withstanding a nuclear blast as close as two miles away. Thus, it would take at least one warhead to disable each missile, even with perfect accuracy. In addition to threatening Soviet targets, the Minuteman system was intended to serve, in case of hostilities, as a sponge to soak up the other side's attacking forces. Missile historian David Baker explains the theory in his book, *The Rocket: The History and Development of Rocket and Missile Technology:*

> The sheer magnitude of the number [of silos] involved would require almost all the Soviet missile forces to be assigned silo targets in the hope that the opposing forces could be diverted from civil and industrial objectives.

The clear, if unspoken, implication of the theory is that the remote and wide open spaces of the Great Plains were to be sacrificed so that California, New

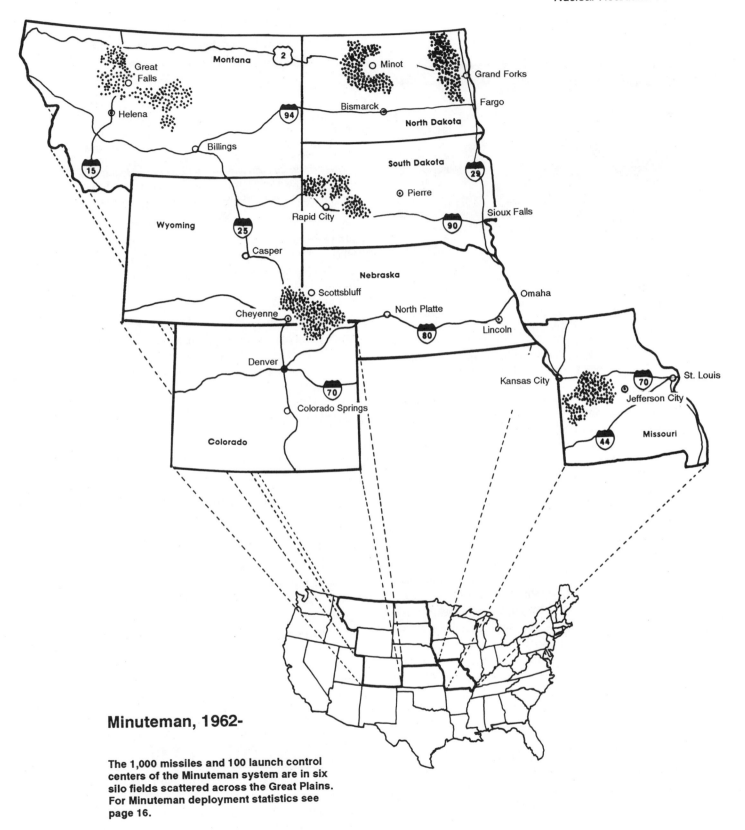

Minuteman, 1962-

The 1,000 missiles and 100 launch control centers of the Minuteman system are in six silo fields scattered across the Great Plains. For Minuteman deployment statistics see page 16.

AP/Wide World

Titan base under construction in Colorado in 1960: An underground city with accommodations for two hundred.

York, Washington D.C., and other centers of more importance to the planners could fight on in a nuclear war. Rather than protecting the safety of those among whom it is deployed, the system actually does the opposite. It enhances their vulnerability, making them the likeliest targets of a Soviet pre-emptive strike if deterrence should fail.

THE THOUSAND MISSILE launch sites now arrayed from northwestern Montana to south central Missouri are the evolutionary product of three decades of strategic conflict. But only on the surface has this been a competition between the United States and the Soviet Union. Underlying the superpower rivalry has been intense domestic struggle: among factions seeking power and leadership in the U.S. Air Force; between the Air Force and the U.S. Navy, its bitter service rival; and among corporate, scientific, and political interests having much at stake in the allocation of money for national defense.

Treated as a stepchild by the military and scientific brass who dominated strategic planning at the end of World War II, ballistic missile development played second fiddle to long-range bombers into the 1950s. German engineers in 1941 had designed a rocket to reach New York and Pittsburgh from the west coast of occupied France but decided the weapon would be impracticable. In 1945 Dr. Vannevar Bush, wartime U.S.

scientific director, derided the idea of an intercontinental ballistic missile:

> The people who have been writing these things that annoy me have been talking about a 3,000-mile, high-angle rocket, shot from one continent to another, carrying an atomic bomb, and so directed as to be a precise weapon, which could land exactly on a certain target, such as a city. I say, technically, I don't think anybody in the world knows how to do such a thing, and I feel confident it will not be done for a very long period of time to come. I wish the American public would leave that out of their thinking.

Despite such discouragement, aerospace think tanks and young Air Force officers with an eye to the future were dreaming up plans for missiles that could hit Moscow.

In 1954, armed with intelligence reports of Soviet research into long-range missiles, the Air Force put a 43-year-old brigadier general, Bernard A. Schriever, in charge of its efforts to build an effective ICBM. Setting up shop in Ingleside, California, as commander of the obscurely titled Western Development Division, he put together a hard-driving staff and began sorting through a welter of competing rocket projects.

At Schriever's prodding, the Joint Chiefs of Staff and National Security Council in 1955 approved a strategic missile master plan, called Weapon System 107, for U.S. entry in the military space race. The primary Air Force strategic missile would be Atlas, a scaled-up version of earlier missiles designed to fly a few hundred miles. Approved as a backup in case problems developed was a similar missile called Titan.

Then, on October 4, 1957, the Soviet launching of Sputnik I, the world's first artificial Earth-orbiting satellite, gave impetus to the U.S. space program. Sputnik's demonstration of Soviet prowess in space technology produced a dizzying profusion of U.S. efforts to catch up. Continuing evidence of a Soviet lead in space, culminating in cosmonaut Yuri Gagarin's pioneering Earth orbit on April 12, 1961, played powerfully into domestic fears of Soviet military supremacy—and into the hands of domestic interests in a position to take advantage of such concerns. Fears of a "missile gap," later shown to be unfounded, became the driving force for one of the most awesome construction efforts—the U.S. military space program—in human history.

Responding to Sputnik, the Air Force rushed Atlas into production. By October 1959 the first six Atlases were in place near Cheyenne, Wyoming. But Atlas was a cumbersome weapon. It took a small army of technicians many hours to raise the missile from its prone position and prepare it for launching. And its fuel was a volatile mix of kerosene and liquid oxygen. Atlas also was vulnerable to attack. A horizontal shelter protected the missile from the weather, but not from the blast of incoming missiles. So, while plunging ahead with deployment of Atlas at a dozen other sites, the Air Force set to work on the backup. Titan's advantage was that it could be launched from an upright underground silo "hardened" against incoming attack and could fling a higher yielding payload (5 megatons—400 times more powerful than the Hiroshima bomb) farther than Atlas.

By the end of 1960 the Air Force had deployed Atlas squadrons (each a small underground city) in Wyoming, Nebraska, Kansas, Washington, California, Oklahoma, Texas, New Mexico, and New York, for a total of 129 missiles, and was in the process of deploying 54 Titans in California, Colorado, Washington, Idaho, and South Dakota.

The typical Titan base was an elaborate complex supporting three missiles in vertical silos, with living accommodations for 200 people, complete with underground power generators, air filtration facilities, sewage treatment units, and chemical waste clarifiers. The cost of the support facilities dwarfed the price of the missiles themselves.

As time went by, new refinements gave rise to new models of Atlas and Titan. Scientists and engineers at the nuclear weapons laboratories devised smaller and lighter warheads, permitting reductions in missile throw-weight. General Electric developed a lighter and tougher non-metallic nose cone which enabled Atlas to fly farther and re-enter the atmosphere with greater speed and precision. Aerojet-General developed a storable liquid fuel which enabled Titan II to remain launch-ready for longer periods.

But, for all the money (about ten billion dollars) thrown into the development of these two missiles and their huge support bases, Atlas and Titan were soon to be doomed by a rival system which set the stage for push-button nuclear war and defined the boundaries of the present missile fields.

Minuteman, named for the figure who symbolized military preparedness in the American revolutionary war, had its genesis in a mixing tank of the Jet Propulsion Laboratory at the California Institute of Technology. In 1946 the lab had produced a highly efficient rocket fuel by adding various chemicals to a

rubbery substance called Thiokol, which previously had been used mainly as a sealant for aircraft fuel tanks. Later, Thiokol Chemical Corp. of Trenton, New Jersey, started making solid fuel power plants for the Army's high-altitude research rockets. The two developments showed that a rocket, powered by a reliable, evenly burning solid fuel, could be launched almost instantly—and by remote control. This presaged the day when launch preparation time (the time it takes a launch crew to corroborate the orders, check all systems, and turn the firing keys), then measured in hours, could be reduced to the one-minute mark. With further refinements, the time eventually would be shaved to the present 31 seconds. (It takes about 30 minutes for the warheads to reach their targets, 6,000 to 7,000 miles away.) In the mid-1950s, with plans for the liquid-fueled Atlas and Titan systems already under way, the implications of Thiokol began to dawn on the Air Force. By 1957, before Sputnik arrived, preliminary plans for Minuteman had been worked out by Space Technology Laboratories (STL), a Los Angeles consulting firm that was to play a key role in developing the new weapon system.

When Sputnik burst on the scene in the fall of 1957, sending shock waves through the U.S. body politic, the Minuteman program was ready to take off. With STL retained as technical consultant, the Air Force assembled a development team made up of Thiokol Chemical Corp., Aerojet-General Corp., and Hercules Powder Co. to manufacture the motors for the rocket's three stages; North American Aviation to build the guidance and control system; Avco Systems to deliver the re-entry vehicle carrying the warhead; and Boeing Airplane Co. to assemble the missile, test it, and build the ground-support equipment. With Boeing as prime contractor, most of these firms or their corporate descendants followed Minuteman's multi-billion-dollar revenue trajectory over the next quarter century.

While portrayed publicly as a way to "catch up with the Russians" in ballistic missile capability, Minuteman was as much the Air Force's attempt to keep up with the U.S. Navy, working hard at that time on a solid-fueled missile of its own, called Polaris, to be launched from submarines. With the Lockheed Corporation as prime contractor for Polaris, the Navy was staking its claim as a major player in the field of strategic deterrence.

But with Minuteman, the Air Force, after many disappointments, had at last found a promising new vehicle for sustained ICBM development. In 1959,

ICBM Deployment, a Chronology

January 1955	Atlas program begins (first U.S. ICBM).
September 1957	Minuteman system proposed.
Oct. 4, 1957	Soviet Union launches Sputnik.
February 1959	First successful test flight of Titan I.
September 1959	First Strategic Air Command ICBM training base set up at Vandenberg AFB, Lompoc, California.
October 1959	First Atlas missiles delivered to F.E. Warren AFB, Cheyenne, Wyoming.
September 1960	Atlas reaches full deployment: 129 missiles at ten bases.
Jan. 20, 1961	President Kennedy takes office.
February 1961	Minuteman I passes full flight test ahead of schedule.
Apr. 12, 1961	Soviet cosmonaut Yuri Gagarin becomes first human to orbit the Earth.
January 1962	Last test flights for Titan I.
May 1962	Titan I operational at five designated bases.
October 1962	First Minuteman flight (ten missiles) operational at Malmstrom AFB, Great Falls, Montana.
October 1962	Cuban missile crisis.
June 1963	First of three Titan II sites ready for use.
July 1963	First Minuteman wing (150 missiles) operational at Malmstrom AFB, Great Falls, Montana.
Nov. 22, 1963	President Johnson takes office after Kennedy assassination.
December 1963	Titan reaches full deployment: 108 missiles at eight bases.
March 1964	Second Minuteman wing operational at Ellsworth AFB, Rapid City, South Dakota.
August 1964	Third Minuteman wing operational at Minot AFB, Minot, North Dakota.
December 1965	Minuteman II wings activated at F.E. Warren AFB, Cheyenne, Wyoming; Whiteman AFB, Knob Noster, Missouri, and Grand Forks AFB, Grand Forks, North Dakota.
April 1967	Fourth Minuteman squadron activated at Malmstrom AFB, Great Falls, Montana, bringing Minuteman total to 1,000.
August 1968	First Minuteman III test fired.
December 1968	Last Atlas missile phased out.
Jan. 20, 1969	President Nixon takes office.
February 1969	Last Minuteman I removed from Malmstrom AFB, Great Falls, Montana.
January 1971	First Minuteman IIIs (multiple warheads) become operational at Minot AFB, Minot, North Dakota.
May 1972	Strategic Arms Limitation Treaty (SALT I) and ABM agreement signed in Moscow.
Aug. 8, 1974	President Ford takes office after Nixon resignation.
July 1975	U.S. reaches planned total of 550 Minuteman IIIs and 450 Minuteman IIs.
Jan. 20, 1977	President Carter takes office.
June 1979	President Carter gives go-ahead on developing MX, a mobile missile with ten warheads.
June 1979	SALT II signed in Vienna (but never ratified by the Senate).
Jan. 20, 1981	President Reagan takes office.
October 1982	First Titan II missiles begin retirement.
December 1986	First ten MX missiles activated in Minuteman missile silos in Wyoming (50 scheduled to be operational by 1990).
June 1987	Last Titan II phased out.

following years of wrangling, the Air Force succeeded in persuading the National Security Council to give it full responsibility for all military space programs, but the edict did nothing to abate competition from the Navy. The two armed services and their affiliated contractors were then just on the threshold of a 30-year war pitting successive generations of Air Force land-based missiles against Navy submarine-launched missiles for strategic pre-eminence. Minuteman and Polaris were the two services' principal entries in the high stakes, big bucks military space race of the 1960s.

Solid fuel, permitting almost instant launching, was the revolutionary engineering component in Minuteman. Equally important in the new weapon concept was its potential for automation—the mass producing of missiles for placement in widely dispersed, simple, secure launch sites requiring relatively little protection or maintenance. This gave promise of a strategic missile force at once more potent and less costly than its predecessors—Atlas and Titan. And that, in turn, attracted the interest of a new space-age President, John F. Kennedy, and his efficiency-minded Secretary of Defense, Robert S. McNamara.

THE MUCH PUBLICIZED "missile gap" was one of the issues that propelled John Kennedy into office in the closely-fought 1960 presidential election. Despite enormous outlays on new space weaponry following Sputnik's first appearance, the Eisenhower Administration seemed in disarray on this issue. Pentagon sources and congressional proponents of a greater military buildup were leaking intelligence reports of fantastic missile progress in the Soviet Union. In one of his many campaign references to the missile gap, addressing an American Legion convention in Miami Beach, Kennedy quoted General Maxwell D. Taylor, later to be chairman of the Joint Chiefs of Staff: "We are now threatened with a missile gap that leaves us in a position of potentially grave danger."

Later, it was to be shown that the United States never had trailed the Soviet Union in missile development. Intelligence estimates showing the U.S. behind dealt only in theoretical Soviet capability. There was never any evidence of Soviet intent to build all the missiles they were capable of building. But these revelations came long after the new president had taken office— and in the meantime he was under pressure to "close the gap." He ordered a step-up in the production of Polaris and doubled Eisenhower's order of Minuteman.

In addition to its technical superiority over Atlas and Titan, Minuteman stood in better grace with the liberal and scientific community, where it was felt the smaller size and lesser yield of Minuteman (barely one megaton in comparison with Atlas/Titan yields of as much as ten megatons) would be less threatening to the Soviets. Even more important to the new Administration, however, was Minuteman's promise of replacing the expensive intermediate-range missile bases that then faced Russia in an arc from Britain through Italy and North Africa to Turkey. Minuteman was also seen as signaling the eventual demise of the expensive long-range bomber. In McNamara's hand it became a lance with which to do battle against the B-70, heir-apparent to the postwar B-52 strategic bomber, much favored by the aging bomber pilots who still dominated the Air Force's higher ranks. Enthralled by the economies and efficiencies inherent in Minuteman, McNamara engaged the Air Force head on, provoking a revolt of the Air Force generals. Led by retired SAC Commander Curtis E. LeMay, many of them backed Senator Barry Goldwater's disastrous presidential campaign of 1964.

If Kennedy needed a clincher for his decision to go full speed ahead with Minuteman, it came on the morning of February 1, 1961, just 12 days after his inauguration. On that day Minuteman passed its first full-scale flight test, scoring a near-bullseye 4,600 miles downrange from Cape Canaveral, enabling the Air Force to lop a full year off its deployment schedule.

Within six months of that spectacular success, the Air Force was breaking ground for Minuteman—at Malmstrom Air Force Base, formerly a bomber refueling station in north central Montana. In July 1962 the first Minuteman missile arrived at Malmstrom, to be followed in succeeding weeks by the placement of nine more missiles in freshly dug silos southeast of Great Falls. It has been said that Alpha 1, launch control center for the first flight of Minutemen, played a role as Kennedy's "ace in the hole" during the Cuban missile crisis of October 1962.

On the day that President Kennedy faced down Chairman Nikita Khrushchev over Soviet missile deployment in Cuba, he could call on 126 Atlas and 54 Titan I ICBMs ready to fire from 16 bases scattered around the United States in addition to his ten new Minutemen. Under construction were another 54 Titan IIs at bases in Arizona, Kansas, and Arkansas. And in the works were five additional bases for another 990 Minutemen.

"For U.S., this is 'the year of the big payoff' in mis-

U.S. ICBM Deployment, 1988

Strategic Missile Wing	Base	Minuteman II*	Minuteman III**	MX***
44th SMW	Ellsworth AFB, SD	150		
90th SMW	F.E. Warren AFB, WY		150	50+
91st SMW	Minot AFB, ND		150	
321st SMW	Grand Forks AFB, ND		150	
341st SMW	Malmstrom AFB, MT	150	50	
351st SMW	Whiteman AFB, MO	150		
	TOTAL	450	500	50

* 1 warhead, 1.2-megaton yield (100 Hiroshimas)
*** 10 warheads, yield up to 300 kilotons each

** 2 or 3 warheads, yield 170 to 350 kilotons each
\+ Deployment of first 50 scheduled for completion by 1990
Source: Nuclear Weapons Databook

siles," trumpeted *U.S. News & World Report* on April 30, 1962. "You see why in this look at a mighty array of long-range weapons that are now in place—ready to fire. And more will be ready soon."

During the last seven months of 1963 ICBMs were coming off U.S. assembly lines at the rate of a missile a day.

On November 22, 1963, when Lyndon Johnson assumed the presidency following the assassination of John Kennedy, all 108 Titan missiles were in place, Minuteman was on line in Montana, North Dakota, and South Dakota; Atlas and Titan I were beginning to be phased out, and Minuteman II (improved range and accuracy) had entered production.

On the heels of first deployment of Minuteman II in October 1965 came the start of development of Minuteman III, containing three smaller warheads, each of which could be aimed at widely separated targets. This marked the arrival of MIRV (multiple independently targeted re-entry vehicles), an ominous new departure vastly increasing the destructive effect of a single missile. The buildup of Minuteman and the phase-out of Atlas and Titan continued through the next four presidencies, with the 1,000th Minuteman going into the ground in July 1975 and the last Titan coming out in June 1987. By that time, 50 Minuteman missile silos were being reconditioned in Wyoming for a new generation of land-based ICBMs—the MX (also known as Peacekeeper), each holding ten MIRVed warheads. Designed as a mobile missile to be launched from trains or trucks, the MX had been approved by the Carter Administration for deployment in the desert of Nevada and Utah. But popular resistance in those states, combined with lobbying from Wyoming, led to a compromise decision to put the first 50 mobile missiles in Minuteman silos in Wyoming. With backing from the Reagan Administration, the Air Force then dusted off an old mobile missile basing plan developed in the 1950s but shelved by President Kennedy. Under "rail garrison," MX would be deployed on specially designed rail cars to be housed in bunkers on air bases and dispersed in time of crisis into the national rail system, where the launch cars would present moving targets. An alternative system, called "Midgetman," preferred by congressional Democrats and liberal "arms control" groups, called for deployment of smaller, single-warhead ICBMs on trucks stationed at Minuteman silos or assigned to drive randomly on military reservations.

PORING ONE DAY through the archives of the late Mayor Oscar Lunseth of Grand Forks, North Dakota, James McKenzie of the University of North Dakota Center for Peace Studies came across a letter to Lence & Englund, a contracting firm in neighboring Minnesota, soliciting funds for a campaign to persuade the Air Force to build a base near Grand Forks. The letter, written in 1954, minced no words:

All of the proposed buildings will directly affect those of us in the building business and, of course, will stimulate all types of business in and around Grand Forks. Your firm is well represented here, and you have become part of the community. I trust that you will be able to contribute to this fund and share with us not only the costs but much of the benefits which will certainly accrue in the months to come.

With or without the financial help of Lence & Englund, and after a tug-of-war with business interests in Fargo, 70 miles to the south, Grand Forks got the fighter base, which later became a base for bombers and missiles of the Strategic Air Command. As is generally the case with military installations and other federal projects, pressure from influential state and local interests sometimes influenced the placement of missile silo bases.

In the late 1950s and early 1960s, when the Air Force was looking for deployment sites that met the needs of Minuteman (light population density, no big cities or vital industry, far enough north to reach Soviet targets), various states and regions competed vigorously for what was viewed as a rich economic prize. It helped to have clout. Missouri enjoyed the influence of Senator Stuart Symington, Secretary of the Air Force under Harry Truman. Wyoming had veteran Senator Gale McGee, a Senate insider renowned for his service to constituents. South Dakota had Senator Karl Mundt, who was well connected in the Eisenhower Administration. And North Dakota had Senator Milton R. Young. Emblematic of Milton Young's influence, a bronze plaque stands today in his native town of LaMoure, North Dakota, expressing the state's gratitude to "a farmer who was selected by his peers to speak their voice in the Halls of Democracy." Standing next to the plaque is a 57-foot Minuteman II.

The monument at LaMoure, repainted from time to time by an Air Force crew, symbolizes the ties that sometimes bind the missile bases and their host regions. Local Air Force Association chapters and chamber of commerce military affairs committees are active in communities adjacent to the missile bases. Local newspapers print reassuring messages.

An editorial in the *Fargo Forum* dated August 28, 1983, repeated a common misconception:

> The United States has vowed it will never fire the first shot in the kind of global battle that could spell what many believe could be the end of civilization as we know it.

From a feature story by editor Steve Trosley of the *Minot Daily News*, February 2, 1988, describing a visit to launch control center D1 near the town of Max, North Dakota:

> Sgt. Brown showed us the place "topside," and when we saw the little stuffed animals in his room, he explained the facility manager's children send out things to make the place more homey and the men like to display the items so the children—who occasionally get to visit—know their dads are thinking about them.

And from an advertisement for the New Testament Baptist Church of Larimore, North Dakota, published in *The Leader,* a newspaper for military personnel and their dependents at Grand Forks Air Force Base:

The LaMoure missile: A monument to an influential U.S. Senator

> We are concerned about where people will spend eternity. It does make a difference where you go to church. Visit us Sunday morning at 10 a.m., where Sunday School is for all ages. A friendly church where the Bible is the final authority. Located 1 block south and 2 blocks west of the Dairy Queen in Larimore.

Over the years the missile silo bases have brought economic sustenance to the cities that adjoin them. The population of Minot, North Dakota, a quiet railroad town, jumped from 22,000 to 33,000 after the Air Force arrived in 1957. The base itself has a population of 13,000. The payroll is about $100-million a year—no small amount to a rural state lacking major industry. The statistics are similar for other towns where missiles are headquartered in North and South Dakota, Missouri, Montana, and Wyoming. Principal beneficiaries are the car dealerships, mobile home courts, restaurants, banks, appliance stores, real estate offices, bowling alleys, and other retail establishments patronized by Air Force personnel and their families. A Great Falls, Montana, Chamber of Commerce brochure glowingly describes the economic and social impact:

> The nerve center of the nation's first Minuteman Missile defense complex, Malmstrom Air Force Base is an "industry" responsible for the employment of 5,375 breadwinners for families in the Great Falls area. Malmstrom's effect on the Great Falls economy translated into dollars amounts to $223.8-million annually. However, its greatest

contribution is the quality and talents of its personnel and their families, who add much to the cultural and civic assets of the city.

Estimates of the economic benefits of missile silo bases usually are derived from data provided by the Air Force. Some believe the estimates are inflated. Silence One Silo, a Montana peace group, challenged an Air Force claim that Malmstrom Air Force Base pumped $255-million into the north central Montana economy in 1985. The organization contended that the Air Force had overstated the ripple effect of many base purchases. Its own calculations showed Cascade County (containing Great Falls) to be the only county in the state benefiting from military spending in 1985. The other counties, including those with missile silos, all received less in military spending than their residents paid in federal taxes going to the military. Silence One Silo's conclusions about the negative net impact of military spending in Montana are reinforced by annual statistical reports of the Department of Defense, showing most of the missile silo states to be among the lowest in the nation in numbers of active and retired military personnel, levels of military spending, and value of military contracts awarded.

Nebraska billboard: The program has failed to make good on its promise.

Construction of the Minuteman launch sites brought thousands of temporary workers to the missile silo states in the late 1950s and early 1960s. But since those boom times the economic benefits of Minuteman have been minimal for the regions where the missiles are deployed. With only a few hundred Air Force personnel needed to control, maintain and guard the 150 to 200 missiles in each field, military spending in the small towns near the launch control centers is next to nothing. It amounts to little more than an occasional stop for hamburgers and gas by Air Force patrol crews. (Air Force spending in the missile silo states is not so much

for operation and maintenance of missiles as for bombers and other aircraft units stationed at missile silo bases.) The highly centralized and automated maintenance system designed for Minuteman a generation ago ensures that any repair work more difficult than the replacement of a component will be taken care of by specialists many hundreds of miles away.

The Air Force continues to spend hundreds of millions of dollars a year to keep Minuteman fine-tuned, but the money goes to factories and military installations far from the missile silo fields. Busiest of these installations are Vandenberg Air Force Base in southern California, flight test center for Minuteman and other missiles, and Hill Air Force Base near Ogden, Utah, where transport planes bring Minuteman and MX in from the field for reconditioning and repair.

While continuing to provide a pay-off for Boeing, Morton-Thiokol and other corporate beneficiaries, Minuteman has failed to make good on its economic promise in missile silo country. The experience of the Morgan County Rural Electrification Association in northeastern Colorado is instructive.

When Minuteman came to Colorado in 1963 the Air Force built 18 launch facilities and a launch control center in Morgan County. In the first year of operation the REA took in more than half a million dollars from the Air Force in hook-up fees and service charges. Later, as costs rose, the REA's domestic and agricultural users found themselves subsidizing the Air Force, which was locked into a low industrial rate. In 1986 the Air Force paid the Morgan County REA 2.85 cents per kilowatt hour, compared with 7 cents charged to some ranchers.

Still more devastating to the ranches, farms and small town businesses of the missile silo states has been the cumulative impact of federal policies inimical to the agricultural economies of those regions. Spending for missile silos and other military programs (close to $300-billion in 1988) has contributed significantly to federal deficits which, by driving up interest rates, have increased the cost of farming at a time when federal policies have kept farm prices down. The disappearance of family farms and the withering away of small farm towns, common in agricultural regions of the United States, is nowhere more evident today than in the missile silo states.

Even in the absence of nuclear war, in which their region would play the part of a national sacrifice area, the people in missile silo country already have paid a high price for being on the front line in the nuclear age.

Chapter II:
The Awakening

"IT'S AMAZING how many people in this state don't even know how many missiles there are," says Mark Anderlik, a peace activist in Montana, where the 200 silos and 20 launch control centers of the 341st Strategic Missile Wing are scattered over thousands of square miles. "It's even more amazing that there are people who live right next to silos and don't even realize it."

Amazing to Mark Anderlik, but not to Jody McLaughlin, whose hometown of Minot, North Dakota, is almost encircled by a vast crescent of 150 nuclear missile silos. "They choose not to know," she says. "The attitude is, 'I don't want to think about it. I don't want to talk about it or acknowledge it.' "

Dr. Tess Rideout, seventh grade counselor at McCormick Junior High School in Cheyenne, Wyoming, headquarters of the 90th Strategic Missile Wing, says, "Around here there are two taboo subjects—sex and nuclear war."

Colonel Kenneth Van Dillen, commander of the 321st Strategic Missile Wing at Grand Forks, North Dakota, once explained to a reporter, "The whole idea behind Minuteman was to be unobtrusively deployed in the middle of a field somewhere and let the agricultural work continue on." One of the missiles his wing controls is in a field farmed by Rueben Rueger near Langdon, North Dakota. "It costs me 35 more minutes to work that field than the other fields," says Rueger. "It's just that many more turns."

Allen Osmundson, who farms near Binford, North Dakota, wrote a letter published by the *Fargo Forum* on March 14, 1987:

> My farm is ringed by three missiles, all less than five miles away, and I worry not at all about that. Whether by nuclear exchange, or by some other method, this earth and these heavens shall pass away with great noise and fervent heat, as 2 Peter 3:10 tells us.

Whether shaped by patriotic pride, fear and intimidation, ignorance, indifference, religious conviction, or

Karen A. Byars

Peace activists record removal of a Minuteman missile to make way for MX in Wyoming: 'We cannot stand idly by...'

day-to-day preoccupation with getting the work done and putting food on the table, stolid acceptance characterizes the general public attitude toward the missile silos of the Great Plains.

But the acceptance is not universal. Even before the first shovel was turned at the first construction site for the first intercontinental ballistic missile, there were protests.

In the winter of 1958 Margaret Laybourn, mother of 11, held up a sign as the lone picket at ceremonies dedicating Francis E. Warren Air Force Base in Cheyenne as a site for Atlas missiles. (Her husband, Robert, a Cheyenne carpenter, had seen the devastation of the atomic bomb as a Marine assigned to clean-up duties at Nagasaki in the aftermath of World War II.)

In 1968 the Rev. Robert Branconnier, Catholic chaplain at the University of North Dakota, stood alone in dissent as spectators gathered for an Air Force test launch at Minuteman missile silo H24 (subsequently dubbed "the fizzle missile" because the rocket failed to leave its underground launch pad).

On April 13, 1982, James Richard Sauder of Little

A gathering at the fence of a North Dakota missile silo.

sat down in the roadway, and one—Kenneth Calkins—was struck by a loaded gravel truck, crushing his left pelvis. The demonstrators, including Calkins, all were jailed for trespassing.

"Appeal to Cheyenne" was an outgrowth of a national movement to raise the level of public concern about nuclear weapons development, then flourishing in the climate of the Cold War. Its leaders included such nationally known figures as Nobel prize-winning biochemist Linus Pauling, pacifist A. J. Muste, and labor leader Bayard Rustin, working through the War Resisters League and other national and international groups. One tactic was to challenge nuclear weapons activity at the source.

On August 6, 1957—12th anniversary of the atomic bombing of Hiroshima—11 protesters were arrested for illegally crossing into Camp Mercury, the nuclear weapons test site in southern Nevada. In 1958, during "Appeal to Cheyenne," two ships, the *Golden Rule* and the *Phoenix*, set sail from Hawaii in attempts to interfere with U.S. atomic testing in the Marshall Islands of the western Pacific. They were stopped by the Coast Guard.

In the summer of 1959, "Omaha Action," a project of the War Resisters League, drew the national spotlight to an Atlas ICBM construction site in eastern Nebraska. A brochure put out by the group summoned Nebraskans and others to take a stand against the missiles:

Rock, Arkansas, climbed the fence of a missile silo in Missouri and conducted a religious service with a cross—for which he paid a penalty of six months in prison.

Only rarely, however, have solitary acts of resistance punctured the numbness toward nuclear arms that generally prevails in missile silo country, as elsewhere in the United States. The missiles are out of sight and out of mind. But occasionally an extraneous development can bring the unseen weapons into public view. Sometimes it is a proposal for deployment of a new missile system, generating intense debate. Or it could be an encounter with some outside group bent on making a point about the evil of nuclear armaments.

The Cheyenne area, site of the nation's initial ICBM deployment, was the scene of the first such encounter. In June 1958 a group organized by a Philadelphia-based pacifist coalition called the Committee for Nonviolent Action drove into Wyoming to conduct what it called "Appeal to Cheyenne," a summer-long effort to persuade local residents to oppose construction of the missile base. They distributed leaflets, talked to reporters, and appeared on radio talk shows, but after two months no visible local support emerged. So the organizers took action themselves. They went out to the construction site to give leaflets to the workers. Some

> At the Omaha ICBM bases—and wherever war preparations go on—indiscriminate suffering and nameless torture are being prepared for countless men, women, and children in our own country and in other lands. We do not want to see our own people so afflicted. We believe that we have no right, under any circumstances, to inflict this evil on another people. We cannot keep silent. We cannot stand idly by or pass on the other side. We hope our words and actions will move others to speak and act for peace.

But missile site construction continued in eastern Nebraska, as it had in the Cheyenne area, without discernible local opposition. The attention of national peace activists shifted the following year to New London, Connecticut, where the Navy was moving into high gear in production of Polaris, the first of its missile-launching submarines. In 1963 the signing of a U.S.-Soviet treaty banning nuclear testing in the atmosphere took much of the political steam out of the "ban the bomb" movement by appearing to diminish nuclear weapons testing, although in fact the agreement merely drove the testing under ground, where it continued at an even brisker pace. By the mid-1960s, as U.S. intercontinental missile deployment approached

Strategic Air Command bases became objects of attention.

Bob Campagna

its zenith, most of the attention and energy previously focused on nuclear arms had shifted to other areas of liberal concern—notably the civil rights movement and the growing U.S. military involvement in Southeast Asia. A long sleep set in while the nuclear weapons buildup continued unhindered.

In the late 1970s and early 1980s critical attention to the missile silos and their supporting air bases began to emerge locally in the missile silo fields—more or less as part of the re-emergence of anti-nuclear peace activism in Europe and the United States.

One of the earliest and most vigorous of these efforts was the Silence One Silo campaign of Montana peace activists. An annual peace camp on the David and

LaVonne Hastings ranch near Conrad, Montana, introduced visitors to R29, a nearby Minuteman III missile silo, where, over several years, a dozen were arrested for climbing over the fence or getting too close to it. Nonsectarian in its approach, Silence One Silo drew on Native American and other spiritual values to reinforce political and economic arguments for nuclear disarmament.

With the blossoming of the nuclear weapons "freeze" movement throughout the United States in 1982-83, ICBM silos and their supporting structures gained a modicum of increased public awareness. Peace gatherings became common occurrences at the gates of missile silo bases in Missouri, Montana, and North and South Dakota. Observances at the fences of the missile silos themselves became traditional at several launch sites in Montana, Nebraska, Colorado, North Dakota, and Missouri. A tree-planting program begun by Larry Lange of Devils Lake called attention to the missile silos in North Dakota. Catholic peace activists in the Omaha area, with heavy input from Catholic Worker Houses in Iowa, began focusing sustained attention on the role of Offutt Air Force Base as the targeting center for the Strategic Air Command. Their vigils at the air base gate were marked by frequent arrests for "crossing the line" onto federal property, often followed by jailings.

Even during the height of renewed concern about nuclear weapons which occured during the first term of the Reagan Administration, it usually took some new development—such as introduction of a new weapon—to stir widespread public thinking about the ICBMs already in the ground. Most notable in this regard was the decade-long controversy over where and how to deploy MX—the mobile land-based ICBM that has been on Air Force drawing boards since 1958. After the Carter Administration's plan for deployment of MX in Utah and Nevada was vociferously rejected by residents of those states, the Reagan Administration settled instead on Wyoming, but not without a hue and

Silo Pruning Hooks(left to right) Fr. Paul Kabat, Helen Dery Woodson, Larry Cloud Morgan, and Fr. Carl Kabat. Opposite page: Their action at Missouri silo N5.

cry from that quarter.

Lindy Kirkbride, mother of three, whose 65,000-acre family ranch near Cheyenne holds three missile silos and a launch control center, was interviewed by a *New York Times* reporter as the first of the new MXs were going into the ground in 1986:

Have you ever been kicked by a horse? In the stomach? That is sort of the feeling I had when they said the [MX] missiles are now on alert.

Her husband, Alan, told *USA Today;*

I sit here, and I think I'm in Utopia... [It] really chaps me when one of our elected public officials begs to get one of these projects in my back yard.

Debates over MX deployment, with national media attention, have illuminated the issues dividing ranchers and farmers from urban interests—real estate developers, retail businesses, banks, school boards, even local symphony orchestras—which see themselves as beneficiaries of local military spending. The debates have also served as reminders of the older silos still present in the nearby countryside. In Wyoming an anti-MX rally drew 400 people to missile silo Q5, just north of Cheyenne. Debates over whether, where,

and how to deploy MX have called attention to the problem of an ever-escalating nuclear arms buildup. But they have not rekindled interest in the missiles presently deployed. It took a more dramatic event to do that.

IN THE EARLY MORNING of November 12, 1984, a yellow station wagon pulling a pneumatic jackhammer mounted on a trailer sped east out of Kansas City, Missouri, on Interstate Highway 70, as if headed for some construction project along that busy transcontinental thoroughfare. At exit 45, near the town of Mayview, it left the main highway, crossed over to the north, and doubled back about half a mile on a service road. Driving up a short gravel road through corn stubble, the vehicle stopped outside a padlocked gate. A man stepped out and cut the chain. As the gate swung open, the station wagon drove through and stopped in front of a large flat slab protruding from the ground—the concrete lid of silo N5, containing a 57-foot Minuteman II missile holding a nuclear warhead a hundred times more powerful than the bomb that destroyed Hiroshima.

Four people had entered the silo enclosure—two Catholic priests in black clerical garb; an Ojibway Indian carrying a multi-colored ceremonial blanket, and a woman wearing a red quilted jacket to ward off the chill. Working deliberately, knowing that they had already set off alarms at a listening post barely a dozen miles away, the four switched on the jackhammer, unloaded sledgehammers and other implements, and started chipping away at the 120-ton steel and concrete cover. Air Force security guards who arrived on the scene about 45 minutes later found the four intruders completing a Christian communion service. Blood had been spattered on the silo superstructure. On the fence had been hung a banner with a quotation from the Old Testament: "Why do you do this evil thing? Your brother's blood cries out to me from the earth."

The symbolic disarming of N5 by the "Silo Pruning Hooks"—the name is taken from the biblical mandate to "beat swords into plowshares and spears into pruning hooks"—focused national attention on missile silos for the first time since the earliest days of the ICBM buildup.

The people who took hammers to silo N5 were Helen Dery Woodson, a writer and political activist from Madison, Wisconsin, whose main occupation had been the rearing of 11 children, one of them her own and the other ten adopted or taken in as foster children,

In cutting the fence, we remove the barriers to peace symbolized there. In pouring our blood, we expose the murderous intent inherent in the weapons and in our government's war policies. In hammering the silo cover and instruments we render temporarily useless a weapon of mass murder, and in damaging the warning system, we express our intent to place our trust in the Lord of Life rather than in 'gods of metal.'

Like other Plowshares activists before them, the Silo Pruning Hooks took an uncompromising position against any and all nuclear weapons; they drew a stark analogy between Nazi mass murders and the holocaust likely to result from the use of nuclear weapons, and they cited legal and scriptural justifications for causing extensive property damage at nuclear weapons sites. Another statement read:

most of them mentally retarded; Fr. Carl Kabat of Madison, an Oblate Catholic priest who had worked with the poor in Brazil and the Philippines; Carl's brother Paul, also an Oblate priest, from Minnesota, and Larry Cloud Morgan, also known as Whitefeather, a mental health worker in Minneapolis. Their visit to N5 was the 11th in a series of "plowshares" actions by peace activists over the preceding four years against military bases, factories, planes, and ships associated with nuclear weapons systems. This was the first directed at a nuclear missile silo. Carl Kabat had participated in two earlier "plowshares" actions, including the first action on September 9, 1980. For the hammering of missile cones in a General Electric factory in King of Prussia, Pennsylvania, he and seven other defendants received sentences of up to ten years.

At N5 the Silo Pruning Hooks left a statement which said:

After the fact, we questioned why people of conscience allowed the slave ships and auction blocks to remain in their midst. After the fact, we insisted that the German people should have cut the fences and torn down the gas chambers and crematoria. After the fact... but there will be no after when the Minuteman missiles have done their demonic work.

Held without bail under a newly enacted federal law designed to deal with terrorists, the Silo Pruning Hooks were charged with destruction of government property, conspiracy, intent to damage the national defense, and trespass. A jury convicted them after a four-day trial. Citing a need to deter others from similar behavior, Federal Judge D. Brook Bartlett handed down the stiffest penalties ever meted out for civil disobedience in the United States. He sentenced Helen Woodson and Carl Kabat to 18 years in prison, Paul

Kabat to ten years, and Larry Cloud Morgan to eight. Later he reduced Carl Kabat's term to ten years and Helen Woodson's to 12 plus five years probation on condition of restitution of the damage—a condition she declared she would not meet. Paul Kabat and Larry Cloud Morgan were released on probation in 1987.

The damage to the missile silo produced consternation not only in government circles but in parts of the peace community as well. Upon hearing complaints that the action had set back the peace movement in Kansas City, Helen Woodson wrote friends:

> People never know the full fruits of their actions, and that is just as well. Conscience is not concerned with 'success' but with right, and too much emphasis on what an act did or did not accomplish shifts the focus from where it belongs. But, if our act has made people unhappy, I can only rejoice in that. Complacent, comfortable, satisfied people do not challenge their assumptions, do not examine their consciences, do not struggle. They are like the frog which sits happily in the ever-increasing heat of the water until he boils.

Whatever other repercussions it may have caused, one of the earliest effects of the Silo Pruning Hooks action was to encourage others to do the same. On the morning of February 19, 1985, just hours before the start of the Pruning Hooks trial, Martin Holladay of Wheelock, Vermont, entered a silo enclosure not far from N5, damaged the lid and some electrical boxes with a hammer and chisel, poured blood, and spray-painted, "No More Hiroshimas." He was charged with crimes similar to those of the Silo Pruning Hooks, convicted, and sentenced to eight years in prison. In his trial before Federal Judge Elmo B. Hunter in Kansas City, in which he represented himself, Holladay sought to illuminate the function and purpose of the "gods of metal" in the soil of western Missouri:

> Mr. Holladay: Do you have any idea if a... nuclear warhead exploded over Kansas City—do you have any idea of the destruction that would result?
> Lt. Pollack: I have no idea.
> Mr. Holladay: You have no idea. So that although you have been trained to launch these missiles, you don't have very much of an idea of what happens when you launch them. Is that correct?
> Lt. Pollack: I don't know the exact things that would happen. But I turn the key, if I have to, and that is my job.
> Mr. Holladay: Has it ever occurred to you how you would feel after you turn the key? Would you feel that you had done your duty, and that is a good thing? Or would you have misgivings?
> Mr. Stewart: I object.

The Court: Sustained.

Judge Hunter and others refused to let nuclear weapons policies be put on trial. Despite the stiff sentences, Plowshares actions against nuclear missile silos continued to occur in Missouri. On Good Friday, 1986, five activists broke into two missile silos and began damaging them with sledgehammers under the gaze of a network television camera crew, invited to film the event. One of them was a 59-year-old grandmother, Jean Gump, from Morton Grove, Illinois, a peace activist for most of her adult years. In sentencing them to terms of seven and eight years, Judge Hunter declared:

> The bottom line is that you did what you did for publicity. You made no effort to take advantage of the many legal ways you had to make your point.

Joe and Jean Gump: God's law over federal law.

In the courtroom audience for Jean Gump's sentencing was her husband Joe, 59, a retired businessman. About a year later, he and Jerry Ebner of Milwaukee, Wisconsin, entered and damaged another Missouri missile silo on the 42nd anniversary of the Hiroshima bombing. Said Joe Gump after his arrest:

> Judge Hunter should understand that the severe sentences he levies to punish and deter such activists will not prevent people of conscience from breaking federal law to obey God's law.

Heavy-handed prosecutorial and judicial reaction to the rising tide of missile silo "disarmament actions" by religiously motivated peace activists prompted Editor Tom Fox to write in the *National Catholic Reporter* on April 18, 1986:

> Try as our nation might to silence resisters, their ranks continue to grow. This is because U.S. policy makers mindlessly pursue destructive courses while many in a contented nation go along. But some day, should humanity survive, voices will ask, Did you speak out? Did you resist? Where were you, the Christian?

HAMMERING ON THE concrete lids of missile silos has done no more than any other peace tactic to diminish the pace of ICBM deployment in the United States. The underground megatonnage continues to mount with each new "Peacekeeper" installed in the rangelands of Wyoming. The Air Force presses on with plans to put new mobile missiles on roads or railroad tracks, ever fearful of a pre-emptive strike on its strategic forces budget by the Navy's newer models of the submarine-launched Trident missile (latest descendant of Polaris). But the Silo Pruning Hooks and their successors have rekindled public interest in the missile silo fields.

The damaging of Missouri missile launch sites has generated other efforts to "reclaim" lands appropriated by the federal government for intercontinental warfare. One example is that of Ladon Sheets.

On May 1, 1986, Ladon Sheets was arrested with two others—Kathy Jennings and Erny Davies—while praying on the lid of missile silo I8, near the Poage Wildlife Area in western Missouri. They did no damage to the missile silo. After serving 23 days in jail, they re-entered the silo enclosure and were sentenced to another five months and 29 days. On Easter Sunday, 1988, Sheets and Jennings placed an Easter lily on the lid of silo L6 at the foot of Bear Butte in South Dakota, a mountain sacred to the Sioux nations. After spending 15 days in jail for that, Sheets prayed on the lid of another South Dakota silo and was sentenced to another 30 days.

The Silo Pruning Hooks action also gave rise to a two-year missile silo mapping project which enlisted the services of scores of volunteers in the seven missile silo states. While the locations of missile silos and launch control centers are well known to the Air Force and the Soviet military through satellite reconnaissance, ordinary Americans until recently had no authoritative guide to these installations. Minuteman missile silos and launch control centers did not appear on any published maps, including official county maps

Aerial view of silo enclosure.

and section maps showing every farm house, barn, and other human structure.

Working from rough data secured by Nukewatch from the U.S. Strategic Air Command, volunteers took to their cars to verify locations of each silo and launch control center and give them names—sometimes humorous, sometimes somber. The first regional map, for Missouri, was completed in the fall of 1985; the last, for South Dakota, rolled off the press in the late summer of 1987. Appearance of the maps usually brought mixed reactions.

Steve Paul of Linton, North Dakota, a retired Air Force security guard, wrote an outraged letter to the *Grand Forks Herald*:

> Maps like this... draw the nuts and crazies like flies to sugar. Do you want to be responsible for causing an 'accident' when someone wants to tamper with a missile site and the security patrol has to do its job protecting the site and may be forced into using deadly force to stop the intruder?

At a Sioux Falls press conference unveiling the South Dakota missile silo map, Tim Langley of the South Dakota Peace & Justice Center contrasted the potential danger to missile silo visitors with the larger danger presented by the missiles themselves:

> We're talking about a tremendous amount of violence and destruction that is waiting to happen. We're trying to identify where these missiles are in our midst, what they do and what has to be done to stop them.

The maps, giving directions to each silo, facilitated the organizing of rallies focusing on missile silos as a local connection with the nuclear arms race. Hundreds attended such a rally on November 9, 1985, at a state park in the midst of the Missouri missile silo field, and many fanned out to spend the night next to nearby missile silos. With permission from the local landowner, it is legal to approach a silo as close as the federal prop-

Susan Nelson

Missouri silo vigil: Helping peace activists get close to the reality of nuclear weapons.

erty line, 25 feet out from the silo fence. Some local farmers not only gave consent but brought food and coffee to the overnight vigilers.

In other ways, the maps have helped peace activists and others get close to the reality of nuclear weapons. A ten-day peace school in the summer of 1987 drew about 250 to a small tent city on Donald Lee's land next to missile silo E46 in North Dakota. In Montana, the Last Chance Peacemakers Coalition of Helena organized tours of the missile silos of Lewis & Clark County. In Missouri, Nancy Thomas of Columbia set up an "Adopt-a-Missile" program in which the adopting parties promise to visit the site regularly and to attempt, through political persuasion, to have the land restored to its original condition.

The mapping of the unattended and widely dispersed Minuteman silos made them accessible for the first time to large numbers for whom nuclear weapons and nuclear warheads are only an abstraction—never seen, never sensed, never experienced. In calling attention to a weapons system long accepted and justified in the name of "nuclear deterrence," the mapping project also challenged the basis of the policy of deterrence.

With nuclear missile silos serving as a focus, the policy of nuclear deterrence can be challenged by legal means, in which gatherings at missile silos stimulate the peace activist, working through the political system, to press for total nuclear disarmament. Or, using hammers and chisels and vials of blood, protesters can utilize nuclear missile silos as instruments for challenging laws which protect weapons and policies of mass destruction. (Presence of an intruder inside a missile silo enclosure is in itself a form of physical and symbolic nuclear disarmament because it is sufficient to take a missile off its "alert" status, if only for an hour or so). Either way, the challenge is not just to the missile, or to a particular class of weaponry, but to nuclear deterrence itself. Each missile silo thus presents an opportunity to advance the cause of nuclear disarmament—an opportunity no farther away than a one-minute walk up a gravel road.

Efforts to call attention to nuclear missile silos offer an alternative to the more conventional approach of "arms control," in liberal vogue since John Kennedy's day, which regards some types of weapons (including Minuteman and Polaris) as acceptable, even desirable, because they are less "de-stabilizing" than others, such as MX, or the anti-ballistic missile, or Star Wars. Nuclear disarmament efforts focusing on Minuteman silos as a point of reference make no such distinctions. They see all nuclear weapon systems as part of the same problem, all rooted in the same dubious policy of threatening to blow up the world to protect the political and economic interests of the United States. As such, the missile silo campaign is more in keeping with the ethical absolutism of the early "ban the bomb" movement, which re-emerged in the 1980s in a variety of forms embodying resistance—legal and illegal—to nuclear weapons *per se*. It is a "new resistance," heavily influenced by religious, spiritual, feminist, and environmental values. It can be seen at "faith and resistance retreats" at the gates of air force bases, at encampments in the Nevada desert where nuclear weapons still are tested, on the railroad tracks leading into Navy submarine bases, and at factories and laboratories deeply interwoven with the nuclear weapons enterprise.

Chapter III
Missile Silos of the United States

THE HIGH PLAINS

The prairie and what's buried underneath it just don't go together. It's important for people to know that there are some people in Cheyenne who are objecting.

—Lorraine Holcomb, Cheyenne school teacher, quoted in *USA Today,* August 29, 1986.

Missile silo D3, near Kimball, Nebraska

© John Hooton

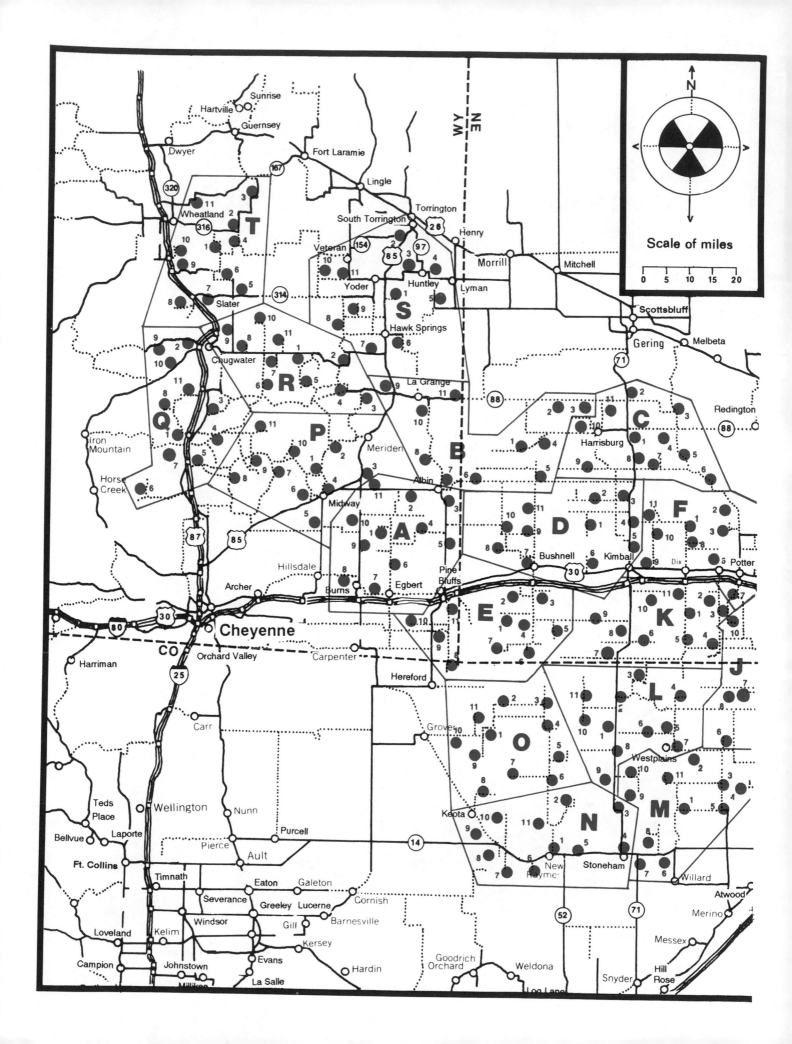

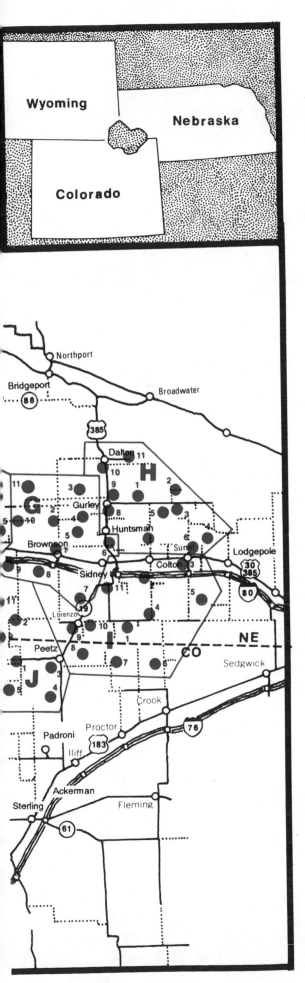

Editor's note: Launch control centers and missile silos on the following pages are identified both by their official Air Force designation and by informal nicknames. The initial letter and number—A1, C3, N39, etc.—are their official names. The informal names were provided for the most part by volunteers who took part in the Nukewatch missile silo mapping project of 1985-1987.

FLIGHT A

A1. Doomsday launch control center. From the grain elevator at Egbert, WY, go north 11.5 miles on County Road 154, then left .5 mile on County Road 223. Control center is on the left.

A2. Life's End missile. From Albin go west 4.9 miles on State Highway 216. Missile is on the left.

A3. Political Objectives missile. From Albin go south 2.4 miles on State Highway 215. Missile is on the left.

A4. Vengeful Aim missile. From Albin go south 7 miles on State Highway 215, then right 4.8 miles on County Road 222. Missile is on the right.

A5. Sequence of Events missile. From Albin go south 8.2 miles on State Highway 215. Missile is on the left.

A6. Moral Disorientation missile. From the grain elevator at Egbert go north 5.3 miles on County Road 154. Missile is on the right.

A7. Outright Insanity missile. From the grain elevator at Egbert go west 2.5 miles on County Road 212. Missile is on the right.

A8. Burns missile. From the railroad tracks in north Burns, go north 1.8 miles on County Road 149 then left 1.5 miles on County Road 215. Missile is on the left.

A9. Annihilation missile. From the railroad tracks in north Burns go north 6.9 miles on County Road 149. Missile is on the right.

A10. Heartbreak missile. From the railroad tracks in north Burns go north 11.2 miles on County Road 149. Missile is on the left.

A11. Pestilence missile. From the junction of U.S. 85 and State Highway 216 north of Midway, go east 6.3 miles on State Highway 216. Missile is on the left.

FLIGHT B

B1. White Tornado launch control center. From the south end of Harrisburg, NE, go west 8.5 miles, then left 6.5 miles. Control center is on the right.

B2. Long Canyon missile. From the junction of State Highways 88 West and 71, go west 13.8 miles. Missile is on the left.

B3. Purple Sage missile. From the junction of State Highways 88 West and 71, go west 8.5 miles. Missile is on the left.

B4. Vogt missile. From the south end of Harrisburg, go west 8.5 miles, then left 1.3 miles. Missile is on the left.

B5. Crooked View missile. From the junction of U.S. 30 and State Highway 53-C at Bushnell, go north 16.7 miles. Missile is on the right.

B6. Lightning Strike missile. From the junction of State Highways 215 and 216 at Albin, go east 2 miles on State Highway 216, then right .3 mile, then right 3.9 miles. Missile is on the left.

B7. Measured Response missile. From Albin, WY, go north 1.4 miles on County Road 162. Missile is on the right.

B8. Bushnell Creek missile. From Albin go north 6.4 miles on County Road 162. Missile is on the left.

B9. Bear Mountain missile. From the junction of U.S. 85 and State Highway 151, go north 1 mile on U.S. 85. Missile is on the left.

B10. Hide the Sun missile. From the railroad tracks at La Grange, go east 1.4 miles on State Highway 151, then right .5 mile. Missile is on the right.

B11. Worldwide Winter missile. From the railroad tracks at La Grange, go east 5.3 miles on State Highway 151. Missile is on the left.

FLIGHT C

C1. Pumpkin launch control center.

Workers practice lowering an MX missile nose cone into a Minuteman silo in Wyoming.

From the junction of State Highway 71 and 88 East, east of Harrisburg, NE, go east .1 mile on State Highway 88. Control center is on the right.

C2. Wildcat Hills missile. From the junction of State Highways 71 and 88 East, east of Harrisburg, go north 6.9 miles on State Highway 71. Missile is on the right.

C3. Prairie Dog missile. From the junction of State Highways 71 and 88 East, east of Harrisburg, go east 8 miles on State Highway 88, then left 4.3 miles. Missile is on the right.

C4. Springs Canyon missile. From the junction of State Highways 71 and 88 East, east of Harrisburg, go east 6.3 miles on State Highway 88. Missile is on the right.

C5. Kirk missile. From the junction of State Highways 71 and 88 East, east of Harrisburg, go east 8 miles on State Highway 88, then right 5.4 miles, then left .4 mile. Missile is on the left.

C6. Lawrence missile. From the junction of State Highways 71 and 88 East, east of Harrisburg, go east 8 miles on State Highway 88, then right 7.2 miles, then left 3.9 miles, then left 1 mile. Missile is on the left.

C7. Indian missile. From the junction of State Highways 71 and 88 East, east of Harrisburg, go south 7.2 miles on State Highway 71, then left 4 miles, then left .2 mile. Missile is on the left.

C8. Jack Rabbit missile. From the junction of State Highways 71 and 88

East, east of Harrisburg, go south 4.8 miles on State Highway 71. Missile is on the left.

C9. Badger missile. From Harrisburg, go south 4.5 miles, then left .3 mile, then right 1 mile, then right 3 miles, then right .4 mile. Missile is on the right.

C10. Willow Creek missile. From the northwest corner of Harrisburg, go west .5 mile, then right 1.6 miles, then left 2.6 miles. Missile is on the left.

C11. Full Moon missile. From the junction of State Highways 71 and 88 West, go west 3.8 miles on State Highway 88. Missile is on the left.

FLIGHT D

D1. Lucifer's launch control center. From the junction of State Highway 71 and U.S. 30 at Kimball, NE, go north 10 miles on State Highway 71, then left 6.7 miles, then left 1.2 miles. Control center is on the left.

D2. Rocky Hollow missile. From the junction of State Highways 71 and 88 East, east of Harrisburg, go south 11.1 miles on State Highway 71, then right 5.9 miles. Missile is on the right.

D3. Snyder missile. From the junction of State Highways 71 and 88 East, east of Harrisburg, go south 10.1 miles on State Highway 71. Missile is on the right.

D4. Dracula's missile. From the junction of U.S. 30 and State Highway 71 at Kimball, go north 8.9 miles on State Highway 71. Missile is on the right.

D5. Kimball's Folly missile. From the junction of U.S. 30 and State Highway 71 at Kimball, go north 4.1 miles on State Highway 71. Missile is on the right.

D6. Ball missile. From the junction of U.S. 30 and State Highway 71 at Kimball, go west 6 miles on U.S. 30,

then right 2.5 miles. Missile is on the right.

D7. Tomich missile. From the junction of U.S. 30 and State Highway 53-C in Bushnell, go north 2 miles. Missile is on the left.

D8. Jeff's missile. From the junction of U.S. 30 and State Highway 53-C at Bushnell, go north 2.3 miles, then left 2 miles, then right 1 mile, then left 2.4 miles. Missile is on the right.

D9. Star missile. From the junction of U.S. 30 and State Highway 53-C at Bushnell, go north 6.3 miles. Missile is on the left.

D10. Elmo Hunter's missile. From the junction of U.S. 30 and State Highway 53-C at Bushnell, go north 2 miles, then left 2 miles, then right 1 mile, then left 2 miles, then right 3 miles, then left 1 mile, then right 1.4 miles. Missile is on the right.

D11. Alderson's Sorrow missile. From the junction of U.S. 30 and State Highway 53-C at Bushnell, go north 10.8 miles. Missile is on the left.

FLIGHT E

E1. Famine launch control center. From the I-80 exit at Bushnell, NE, go south 6 miles, then right 4.6 miles. Control center is on the left.

E2. Starving Children missile. From the I-80 exit at Bushnell go south 2 miles, then right 2 miles, then right .8 mile. Missile is on the left.

E3. Fateful Question missile. From the I-80 exit at Bushnell, go .9 mile south, then left 2.9 miles. Missile is on the right.

E4. Killer missile. From the I-80 exit at Bushnell, go south 6.1 miles, Missile is on the right.

E5. Imperialist missile. From the I-80 exit at Bushnell, go south 7 miles, then left 4.1 miles, then right 1.5 miles. Missile is on the left.

E6. Sam's missile. From the I-80 exit at Bushnell, go south 10 miles, then right .2 mile, then left .6 mile. Missile is on the left.

E7. Strangelove missile. From the I-80 exit at Bushnell, go south 10 miles, then right 4.2 miles, then left 1 mile, then right .8 mile. Missile is on the right.

E8. Tri-State missile. From the

junction of U.S. 30 and Beech Street on the east side of Pine Bluffs, WY, go south 12.5 miles. Missile is on the left.

E9. Nixon's missile. from the junction of U.S. 30 and Beech Street on the east side of Pine Bluffs, go south 7.7 miles, then right .3 mile. Missile is on the left.

E10. Muddy Creek missile. From the junction of U.S. 30 and Beech Street on the east side of Pine Bluffs, go south 6.9 miles, then right 6.3 miles on County Road 206. Missile is on the right.

E11. Pine Bluffs missile. from the junction of U.S. 30 and Beech Street on the east side of Pine Bluffs, go south 3.3 miles. Missile is on the left.

FLIGHT F

F1. Hardened Criminal launch control center. From the junction of U.S. 30 and 53-A Link at Dix, NE, go north 8.9 miles. Control center is on the right.

F2. Greed missile. From the junction of U.S. 30 and 17-B Link at Potter, go north 12 miles, then left 3 miles, then right .7 mile. Missile is on the left.

F3. George Schultz's missile. From the junction of U.S. 30 and 17-B Link at Potter, go north 8.3 miles, then left 1 mile, then right .1 mile. Missile is on the left.

F4. Perversity missile. From the junction of U.S. 30 and 17-B Link at Potter, go north 7.3 miles, then right 4 miles. Missile is on the left.

F5. Buffalo missile. From Potter, go east 2 miles on U.S. 30, then left 1.5 miles, then right .5 mile, then left 1 mile. Missile is on the right.

F6. Killing Fields missile. From the junction of U.S. 30 and 53-A Link at Dix, go north 3 miles, then right 5 miles. Missile is on the right.

F7. Obscenity missile. From the junction of U.S. 30 and 17-B Link at Potter, go south 1.2 miles. Missile is on the right.

F8. Secret Fallout missile. From the junction of U.S. 30 and 53-A Link at Dix, go north 4 miles, then right .4 mile. Missile is on the left.

F9. Bennett missile. From the junc-

Karen A. Byars

Peace activists meet security guard at an MX silo construction site in Wyoming. Set aside for MX missiles are 50 silos in Flights P, Q, R, S and T.

tion of State Highway 71 and U.S. 30 at Kimball, go east 4 miles on U.S. 30, then left 1.9 miles. Missile is on the left.

F10. Rose missile. From the junction of State Highway 71 and U.S. 30 at Kimball, go east 4 miles on U.S. 30, then left 6.7 miles. Missile is on the right.

F11. Ostgren missile. From the junction of State Highway 71 and U.S. 30 at Kimball, go east 4 miles on U.S. 30, then left 8.9 miles, then right 1 mile, then left 3 miles. Missile is on the left.

FLIGHT G

G1. Western Nebraska Community College launch control center. From the junction of U.S. 30 and 17-A Spur at Brownson, NE, go south .3 mile on 17-A Spur, then right 2.1 miles on 17-A Spur, then right .5 mile through WNCC campus. Control center is on the right.

G2. Ordville missile. From the

junction of U.S. 30 and 17-A Spur at Brownson, go south .3 mile on 17-A Spur, then right 7.5 miles on 17-A Spur, then right 1.1 mile. Missile is on the right.

G3. Kriesel missile. From the north end of Gurley, go north 2 miles on U.S. 385, then left 3.4 miles. Missile is on the right.

G4. Discovery missile. From the north end of Gurley, go south 2 miles on U.S. 385, then right 1.1 miles. Missile is on the left.

G5. Hunts Humans missile. From Huntsman go west 1 mile, then right .2 mile. Missile is on the left.

G6. Total War missile. From the junction of U.S. 385 and U.S. 30 east of Sidney, go north 3.5 miles on U.S. 385, then right .7 mile, then right 1 mile, then left 2.3 miles. Missile is on the left.

G7. Airport missile. From Lorenzo, go northeast 3.8 miles on State Highway 19. Missile is on the right.

G8. Contaminated Forevermore

missile. From the junction of U.S. 30 and 17-A Spur at Brownson, go east .6 mile on U.S. 30, then right 2.7 miles. Missile is on the right.

G9. Earl missile. from the junction of U.S. 30 and 17-B Link at Potter, go east 4.5 miles on U.S. 30, then right 2.3 miles. Missile is on the left.

G10. Water Hole missile. From the junction of U.S. 30 and 17-B Link at Potter, go north 4.5 miles, then right 7.9 miles. Missile is on the right.

G11. Maas missile. From the north end of Gurley, go north 2 miles on U.S. 385, then left 8 miles. Missile is on the right.

FLIGHT H

H1. Oil Tank launch control center. From the north end of Gurley, NE, go east 7.5 miles. Control center is on the left.

H2. Nowhere missile. From the north end of Gurley, go east 10.8 miles, then left 3 miles, then right .6 mile. Missile is at dead end.

H3. Dorman missile. From the north end of Gurley go east 15 miles, then right .8 mile. Missile is on the right.

H4. Rush missile. From the west end of Lodgepole, go north 5.8 miles, then left 1 mile. Missile is on the left.

H5. Spearow missile. From Sunol, go north 8.3 miles, then left 1 mile. Missile is on the right.

H6. Grandview missile. From the west end of Lodgepole, go west 3.9 miles on U.S. 30, then right 2.2 miles on Weyetga Road. Missile is on the right.

H7. Johnson missile. From the junction of U.S. 30 and Colton Road, go east 3.2 miles on U.S. 30, then left 3.5 miles, then left .8 mile. Missile is on the right.

H8. Xenia missile. From Huntsman, go north 2 miles on U.S. 385, then right 3 miles. Missile is on the left.

H9. Pope missile. From the north end of Gurley, go east 3 miles. Missile is on the left.

H10. Damned missile. From Dalton go south .7 mile on U.S. 385, then east .6 mile. Missile is on the right.

H11. Anderson missile. From Dalton, go south .7 mile on U.S. 385, then left 5.4 miles. Missile is on the left.

FLIGHT I

I1. Bad Faith launch control center. From Lorenzo, NE, go east 10.4 miles, then right .3 mile. Control center is on the left.

I2. Flash! -- Boom! missile. From the junction of U.S. 30 and U.S. 385 northeast of Sidney, go east 4.5 miles, then south 3.3 miles, then left 1.5 miles. Missile is on the left.

I3. Blood and Ashes missile. From the west end of Lodgepole, go west 4 miles on U.S. 30, then left 2.3 miles. Missile is on the right.

I4. Lone missile. From Lorenzo go east 15.2 miles. Missile is on the left.

I5. Jeannette Rankin missile. From Lodgepole, go south 6.7 miles on L-17-F, then right 3 miles. Missile is on the right.

I6. Junkies of Hate missile. From Crook, CO, go north 3.5 miles on County Road 81, then left 1 mile, then right 5 miles, then right .7 mile. Missile is on the right.

I7. Industrial Waste missile. From Proctor, go northeast 2.8 miles on U.S. 138, then left 10.8 miles on County Road 71. Missile is on the left.

I8. Incredible Deterrent missile. From Proctor go west .5 mile, then right 5.8 miles on County Road 65, then left 1 mile on County Road 62, then right 5.8 miles on County Road 63, then left 1 mile on County Road 72, then right 1.5 miles on County Road 61. Missile is on the left.

I9. Escalation missile. From Lorenzo, NE, go east .4 mile, then right 1 mile. Missile is on the left.

I10. Blind Faith missile. From Lorenzo, go east 5.4 miles, then right .5 mile. Missile is on the right.

I11. Cow Creek missile. From the junction of U.S. 30 and U.S. 385 east of Sidney, go south 3 miles on L-17-J, then left 1.9 miles at a "T", then right .3 mile. Missile is on the right.

FLIGHT J

J1. Emotionally Suffocating launch control center. From Peetz, CO, go west 5 miles. Control center is on the left.

J2. Patriarch's missile. From the junction of U.S. 30 and 17-B Link at Potter, NE, go east 4.5 miles on U.S. 30, then right (over I-80) 11.2 miles, then left 3.6 mile. Missile is on the right.

J3. Good Friday missile. From Peetz, go south 1.5 miles on State Highway 113. Missile is on the left.

J4. Ellanor's missile. From Peetz, go south 6.3 miles on State Highway 113. Missile is on the left.

J5. Killing Us Softly missile. From Peetz, go west 6 miles, then left 5.9 miles. Missile is on the left.

J6. Bob's missile. From the west junction of State Highways 71 & 14, go north 20.1 miles on State Highway 71, then right 10.2 miles on County Road 124, then right 3 miles, then left 7.9 miles, then left 3 miles on County Road 25. Missile is on the right.

J7. Damned If You Do missile. From Peetz, go west 6 miles, then left 1 mile, then right 3 miles. Missile is on the right.

J8. Ed's missile. From Peetz, go west 13.5 miles. Missile is on the left.

J9. Apocalypse missile. From Peetz, go west 6 miles, then right 3.6 miles on County Road 37, then left 2.5 miles. Missile is on the right.

J10. Armageddon missile. From the junction of U.S. 30 and 17-B Link at Potter, NE, go south 3 miles, then right 8 miles, then left 2 miles. Missile is on the left.

J11. Dead End missile. from the junction of U.S. 30 and 17-B Link at Potter, go east 4.5 miles on U.S. 30, then right (over I-80) 8.2 miles, then right .3 mile. Missile is on the left.

FLIGHT K

K1. Genocide launch control center. From the junction of U.S. 30 and 53-A Link at Dix, NE, go south 6.7 miles. Control center is on the left.

K2. Potter South missile. From the junction of U.S. 30 and the 17-B Link at Potter, go west 4.2 miles on U.S. 30, then left 3.1 miles (over I-80), then right .9 mile. Missile is on the left.

K3. Acid rain missile. From the junction of U.S. 30 and the 17-B Link at Potter, go west 4.2 miles on U.S. 30, then left 8.2 miles (over I-80). Missile is on the left.

K4. Dead Prairie Dog missile. From the junction of U.S. 30 and the 17-B Link at Potter, go west 4.2 miles

Olive branch in a mailed fist: official emblem of the Strategic Air Command.

on U.S. 30, then left 13.3 miles (over I-80). Missile is on the right.

K5. Road's End missile. From the junction of U.S. 30 and 53-A Link at Dix, go south 11.4 miles. Missile is on the left.

K6. Final Deluge missile. From the I-80 exit at Kimball, go south 9.6 miles on State Highway 71, then left 3.6 miles. Missile is on the left.

K7. Cold War missile. From the I-80 exit at Kimball, go south 10.6 miles on State Highway 71, then right 2 miles. Missile is on the left.

K8. The Generic missile. From the I-80 exit at Kimball, go south 6.5 miles on State Highway 71. Missile is on the right.

K9. Hawk missile. From the I-80 exit at Kimball, go south 5.6 miles on State Highway 71, then right 5.2 miles. Missile is on the right.

K10. Slim Chance missile. From the I-80 exit at Kimball, go south 1.6 miles on State Highway 71, then left 4.1 miles. Missile is on the right.

K11. Dix's Folly missile. From the junction of U.S. 30 and 53-A Link at Dix, go south 1.2 miles. Missile is on the right.

FLIGHT L

L1. Kathy's launch control center. From the west junction of State Highways 71 and 14, go north 22.2 miles on State Highway 71. Control center is on the left.

L2. The Real Terror Network missile. From the west junction of State Highways 71 and 14, go north 27 miles on State Highway 71. Missile is on the right.

L3. Colo-Neb missile. From the junction of I-80 and State Highway 71 at Kimball, NE, go south 13 miles on State Highway 71, then left 5 miles, then right 2.5 miles. Missile is on the right.

L4. Accidents Happen missile. From the west junction of State Highways 71 and 14, go north 20.1 miles on State Highway 71, then right 10.2 miles on County Road 124, then left 7 miles, then right 1.3 miles. Missile is on the left.

L5. Shared Fate missile. From the west junction of State Highways 71 and 14, go north 20.1 miles on State Highway 71, then right 10.2 miles on County Road 124, then left 2.4 miles. Missile is on the left.

L6. With Malice Aforethought missile. From the west junction of State Highways 71 and 14, go north 20.1 miles on State Highway 71, then right 6 miles on County Road 124. Missile is on the left.

L7. Maniacal missile. From the west junction of State Highways 71 and 14, go north 20.1 miles on State Highway 71, then right 10.2 miles on County Road 124, then right 2.8 miles. Missile is on the left.

L8. Caspar's missile. From the west junction of State Highways 71 and 14, go north 17.7 miles on State Highway 71. Missile is on the right.

L9. Koyaanisqatsi missile. From the west junction of State Highways 71 and 14, go north 13.3 miles on State Highway 71. Missile is on the left.

L10. Random and Senseless missile. From the west junction of State Highways 71 and 14, go north 24 miles on State Highway 71, then left 5 miles on County Road 132, then left 2 miles, Missile is on the left.

L11. Lone Assassin missile. From the west junction of State Highways 71 and 14, go north 24 miles on State Highway 71, then left 5 miles on County Road 132, then right 3.5 miles on County Road 135. Missile is on the right.

FLIGHT M

M1. Wild Horse Lake launch control center. From the junction of State Highway 14 and U.S. 6 at Sterling, CO, go west 7.6 miles on U.S. 14, then right 5.3 miles on County Road 25, then left 6.5 miles on County Road 38. Control center is on the right.

M2. Ron's missile. From the west junction of State Highways 71 and 14, go north 20.1 miles on State Highway 71, then right 10.2 miles on County Road 124, then east 10.2 miles on County Road 124, then right 3 miles, then left 4.9 miles. Missile is on the right.

M3. Nancy's missile. From the junction of State Highway 14 and U.S. 6 at Sterling, go west 7.6 miles on State Highway 14, then right 5.3 miles on County Road 25, then left 1.6 miles on County Road 38, then right 5.5 miles. Missile is on the right.

M4. Dirty War missile. From the junction of U.S. 138 and the Padroni Road (.1 mile north of the railroad tracks northeast of Sterling), go north 6.4 miles on the Padroni Road, then left 3 miles, then right 4 miles on County Road 37, then left 3 miles on County Road 54, then right .1 mile. Missile is on the left.

M5. Misanthropic missile. From the junction of State Highway 14 and U.S. 6 at Sterling, go west 7.6 miles on State Highway 14, then right 5.3

miles on County Road 25, then left 1.3 miles on County Road 38. Missile is on the right.

M6. Misbegotten missile. From the west junction of State Highways 71 and 14, go east 9 miles on State Highway 14. Missile is on the right.

M7. Miscreant missile. From the west junction of State Highways 71 and 14, go east 3.8 miles on State Highway 14. Missile is on the right.

M8. Colossal Misprision missile. From the west junction of State Highways 71 and 14, go east 6.8 miles on State Highway 14, then left 3.9 miles on County Road 5, then left .4 mile on County Road 34. Missile is on the left.

M9. Kenneth Calkins missile. From the west junction of State Highways 71 and 14, go north 14.1 miles on State Highway 71, then right 4 miles on County Road 112, then right 3.8 miles. Missile is on the right.

M10. Ted Olson's missile. From the west junction of State Highways 71 and 14, go north 14.1 miles on State Highway 71, then right 4 miles on County Road 112, then left .4 mile. Missile is on the left.

M11. Misappropriated missile. From the junction of State Highway 14 and U.S. 6 at Sterling, go west 7.6 miles on State Highway 14, then right 5.3 miles on County Road 25, then left 6.5 miles on County Road 38, then right 4 miles on County Road 11, then left 2 miles on County Road 46, then right 1.6 miles on County Road 7. Missile is on the right.

FLIGHT N

N1. Bill Armstrong's launch control center. From the junction of State Highway 14 and County Road 129 at New Raymer, CO, go north 1.6 miles on County Road 129. Control center is on the right.

N2. Pat Schroeder's missile. From the junction of State Highway 14 and County Road 129 at New Raymer, go north 4 miles on County Road 129, then right 2.2 miles, then left 1.1 miles, then right 3.5 miles, making frequent turns. Missile is on the left.

N3. Gary Hart's missile. From the west junction of State Highways 71 and 14, go north 7.5 miles on State Highway 71. Missile is on the right.

N4. Dan Schaefer's missile. From the west junction of State Highways 71 and 14, go north 2.2 miles on State Highway 71. Missile is on the right.

N5. Ken Kramer's missile. From New Raymer, go east 4 miles on State Highway 14. Missile is on the left.

N6. Tim Wirth's missile. From New Raymer, go west 3 miles on State Highway 14, then left .4 mile on County Road 123. Missile is on the left.

N7. Dick Lamm's missile. From New Raymer, go west 8.2 miles on State Highway 14, then left 3.8 miles on County Road 115. Missile is on the left.

N8. Hank Brown's missile. From New Raymer, go west 9.3 miles on State Highway 14, then left .2 mile on County Road 113. Missile is on the right.

N9. Mike Strang's missile. From the junction of State Highway 14 and County Road 390, go northwest 3.7 miles on County Road 390. Missile is on the left.

N10. Steve Slaton's missile. From New Raymer, go west 8.2 miles on State Highway 14, then right 5.3 miles on County Road 115. Missile is on the left.

N11. Hal Johnson's missile. From the junction of State Highway 14 and County Road 129 at New Raymer, go north 4 miles on County Road 129, then left 2.6 miles. Missile is on the left.

FLIGHT O

O1. Hammer of Hell launch control center. From Grover, CO, go east 9 miles on County Road 122, then left 1 mile on County Road 107, then right 2 miles on County Road 124. Control center is on the right.

O2. Crying Children missile. From Grover, go east 9 miles on County road 122, then left 1 mile on County Road 107, then right 2 miles on County Road 124, then left 5 miles on County Road 111, then right 2.5 miles on County Road 134. Missile is on the left.

O3. Starvation missile. From the junction of State Highway 14 and

County Road 129 at New Raymer, go north 4 miles on County Road 129, then left 16 miles on County Road 129/127, then left .5 mile on County Road 124, then right 2.3 miles, then right 3 miles. Missile is on the right.

O4. Famine missile. From the junction of State Highway 14 and County Road 129 at New Raymer, go north 4 miles on County Road 129, then left 16 miles on County Road 129/127, then left .5 mile on County Road 124, then right .3 mile. Missile is on the right.

O5. Lamentation missile. From the junction of State Highway 14 and County Road 129 at New Raymer, go north 4 miles on County Road 129, then left 11.8 miles on County Road 129, then right 3.2 miles on County Road 116, then left .7 mile. Missile is on the left.

O6. Agony missile. From the junction of State Highway 14 and County Road 129 at New Raymer, go north 4 miles on County Road 129, then left 8.6 miles on County Road 129/127. Missile is on the right.

O7. Calamity missile. From the junction of State Highway 14 and County Road 129 at New Raymer, go north 4 miles on County Road 129, then left 8.8 miles on County Road 129, then left 5.8 miles on County Road 110. Missile is on the right.

O8. Fire Storm missile. From Keota, go north 3 miles on County Road 105, then right 2.2 miles on County Road 104. Missile is on the left.

O9. Ground Burst missile. From Grover, go east 9 miles on County Road 122, then right 3.5 miles. Missile is on the right.

O10. Malediction missile. From Grover, go east 6 miles on County Road 122. Missile is on the right.

O11. Malevolent missile. From Grover go east 8 miles on County Road 122, then left 3.8 miles on County Road 105. Missile is on the right.

FLIGHT P

P1. Little Horse Creek launch control center. From the junction of U.S. 85 and County Road 143 at Midway,

WY, go north 5 miles on County Road 143. Control center is on the left.

P2. Ed Herschler's missile. From the junction of U.S. 85 and County Road 143 at Midway, go north 10 miles on County Road 143. Missile is on the right.

P3. Herrick Creek missile. From the junction of U.S. 85 and State Highway 216 East, go northeast 5.4 miles on U.S. 85. Missile is on the right.

P4. Malcolm Wallop's missile. From the junction of U.S. 85 and County Road 143 at Midway, go north 1.4 miles on U.S. 85. Missile is on the left.

P5. Chevington Draw missile. From the junction of U.S. 85 and County Road 143 at Midway, go south 5 miles on County Road 143. Missile is on the right.

P6. Alan K. Simpson's missile. From the junction of U.S. 85 and County Road 143 at Midway, go southwest 4.5 miles on U.S. 85, then right 1.3 miles on County Road 139. Missile is on the left.

P7. Wacker Draw missile. From the junction of U.S. 85 and County Road 143 at Midway, go north 4.9 miles on County Road 143, then left 2.5 miles on County Road 232, then right 2 miles, then left 1.8 miles, then left 3.4 miles on County Road 233, then left 1.7 miles on County Road 132. Missile is on the left.

P8. Horse Creek East missile. From I-25 Exit 34, go south .7 mile on the frontage road, then left 2.4 miles, then right 5 miles. Missile is on the left.

P9. Mutation missile. From I-25 Exit 34, go south .7 mile on the frontage road, then left 2.4 miles, then right 5 miles, then left 2 miles, then right 3 miles, then left 1 mile. Missile is on the right.

P10. Les Aspin's missile. From the junction of U.S. 85 and County Road 143 at Midway, go north 4.9 miles on County Road 143, then left 2.5 miles on County Road 232, then right 2 miles, then left 1.8 miles, then right 1.6 miles on County Road 233. Missile is on the right.

P11. Lost Hope missile. From I-25 Exit 39, go north 1.5 miles on the frontage road, then right 9.3 miles, then forward 2.5 miles. Missile is on the left.

FLIGHT Q

Q1. Bear Creek launch control center. From I-25 Exit 39, go southwest .5 mile on County Road 237-A. Control center is on the left.

Q2. Air Burst missile. From I-25 Exit 54, go west 2 miles on Diamond Ranch road. Missile is on the left.

Q3. Frightful Effects missile. From I-25 Exit 47, go south 1 mile on the west frontage road, then left .2 mile, then right 2.6 miles, then left .6 mile. Missile is on the left.

Q4. Double Vision missile. From I-25 Exit 39, go north 1.5 miles on the east frontage road, then right 3.6 miles on County Road 238. Missile is on the right.

Q5. Remain Calm missile. From I-25 Exit 34, the Nimmo road, go south .5 mile on the frontage road, then left .8 mile on County Road 232. Missile is on the left.

Q6. Military Xenophobia missile. From I-25 Exit 29, go west 7.5 miles on County Road 228, then right 1.5 miles. Missile is on the left.

Q7. Bristol Ridge Road missile. From I-25 Exit 39, go south 1.6 miles on the east frontage road, then right 4.6 miles on County Road 237. Missile is on the left.

Q8. Chalk Hill missile. From I-25 Exit 47, go south 1 mile on the west frontage road, then right 4.7 miles, then left 2 miles, then right 2 miles, then left .9 mile. Missile is on the right.

Q9. Global Damage missile. From I-25 Exit 54, go west 7 miles on Diamond Ranch Road. Missile is on the left.

Q10. Radioactive Rain missile. From I-25 Exit 54, go southwest 6.7 miles on Iron Mountain Road. Missile is on the right.

Q11. Chugwater Creek missile. From I-25 Exit 47, go south 1.1 miles on the west frontage road, then right 3.5 miles on County Road 244. Missile is on the right.

FLIGHT R

R1. County Commissioners' launch control center. From the railroad tracks at Chugwater, go east 16.5 miles on State Highway 313. Control center is on the right.

R2. Castle Rocks missile. From Hawk Springs, go south 3 miles on U.S. 85, then right 8.5 miles on State Highway 313. Missile is on the right.

R3. Phillips missile. From the junction of U.S. 85 and State Highway 151, go west 5.6 miles on State Highway 151, then left .9 mile. Missile is on the left.

R4. Diamond Flats missile. From the junction of U.S. 85 and State Highway 151, go west 8.6 miles, then right 2 miles, then left .4 mile. Missile is on the left.

R5. Ignorance missile. From the junction of U.S. 85 and State Highway 151, go west 8.6 miles on State Highway 151, then right 2 miles, then left 7.2 miles (past R4). Missile is on the right.

R6. Buy or Die missile. From the railroad tracks at Chugwater, go east 8.9 miles on State Highway 313, then right 5.9 miles along power line. Missile is on the left.

R7. Pol Pot missile. From the railroad tracks at Chugwater, go east 10.8 miles on State Highway 313, then right 1.5 miles. Missile is on the right.

R8. Authoritarian missile. From the railroad tracks at Chugwater, go east 7 miles on State Highway 313, then left 1 mile. Missile is on the left.

R9. Totalitarian missile. From the railroad tracks at Chugwater, go east 4.1 miles on State Highway 313, then left 4.3 miles. Missile is on the left.

R10. Burning Wound missile. From the railroad tracks at Chugwater, go east 8.9 miles on State Highway 313, then left 5 miles along power line, then left .5 mile. Missile is on the right.

R11. Goshen Hole Rim missile. From the railroad tracks at Chugwater, go east 12.6 miles on State Highway 313, then left 3 miles. Missile is on the left.

FLIGHT S

S1. Laramie Canal launch control center. From Hawk Springs, go north 6 miles on U.S. 85, then right 2.3 miles, Control center is on the left.

S2. Headbanger missile. From the North Platte River at Torrington, go south 2.3 miles on U.S. 85. Missile is on the right

S3. Pornographic missile. From the junction of State Highways 92 and 161 south of Huntley, go west 2.6 miles on State Highway 161. Missile is on the right.

S4. Misogynist missile. From the junction of State Highways 92 and 161 south of Huntley, go east .8 mile on State Highway 92, then continue east 2 miles. Missile is on the left.

S5. Table Mountain missile. From the junction of State Highways 92 and 161 south of Huntley, go east and south 2.8 miles on State Highway 92, then right 3.9 miles on State Highway 158, then left .9 mile. Missile is on the left.

S6. Present Danger missile. From Hawk Springs, go east 3 miles, then right .5 mile. Missile is on the right.

S7. Only One Earth missile. From Hawk Springs, go south 3 miles on U.S. 85, then right 2.4 miles on State Highway 313. Missile is on the right.

S8. Friendly Fascism missile. From Hawk Springs, go north 3 miles on U.S. 85, then left 6.9 miles, then left 2 miles. Missile is on the right.

S9. Stoking Ovens missile. From Hawk Springs, go north 3 miles on U.S. 85, then left 4.9 miles, then right 1.6 miles. Missile is on the left.

S10. Red Bill Hill missile. From the water tower at Yoder, go west 4.4 miles on State Highway 154, then continue west 5.2 miles, then right 1.8 miles. Missile is on the right.

S11. Rivers of Blood missile. From the water tower at Yoder, go west 4.4 miles on State Highway 154, then right .2 mile. Missile is on the left.

FLIGHT T

T1. Macabre Experiment launch control center. From the junction of Business I-25 and State Highway 316 at Wheatland, go east 7.7 miles on State Highway 316, then right 3.5 miles. Control center is on the right.

T2. Eagle's Nest missile. From the junction of Business I-25 and State Highway 316 at Wheatland, go east 12.6 miles on State Highway 316. Missile is on the left.

T3. Deer Creek missile. From the junction of Business I-25 and State Highway 316 at Wheatland, go east 21.7 miles on State Highway 316. Missile is on the left.

T4. Magistrate's Extrajudicial missile. From the junction of Business I-25 and State Highway 316 at Wheatland, go east 11.5 miles on State Highway 316, then right 3.6 miles. Missile is on the right.

T5. Munition Execrable missile. From I-25 Exit 65, go east 7.5 miles on Slater Road/State Highway 314. Missile is on the left.

T6. Mandatory Exode missile. From I-25 Exit 65, go east 6.4 miles on Slater Road/State Highway 314, then left 3 miles on State Highway 315, then left 2.8 miles on Bordeaux Road. Missile is on the right.

T7. Mangled Exit missile. From I-25 Exit 65, go east 2.3 miles on Slater Road/State Highway 314. Missile is on the right.

T8. Mussolini's Exile missile. From I-25 Exit 65, go south 1 mile on Richeau Road, then right 2 miles. Missile is on the right.

T9. Antelope Creek missile. From I-25 Exit 70, go east .4 mile on Bordeaux Road. Missile is on the left.

T10. Magnified Exploitation missile. From I-25 Exit 73, go north 2.7 miles on the east frontage road, then right .3 mile. Missile is on the right.

T11. Masculine Excrescence missile. From the junction of Business I-25 and State Highway 320 (North Wheatland Highway) at Wheatland, go north 2.3 miles on State Highway 320, then right 4.6 miles on Gray Rocks Road. Missile is on the right.

High Plains Silos of Note

C2. Site of an annual Hiroshima Day (August 6) observance by western Nebraska peace activists. Participants walk to the silo from Wildcat State Park, 1.5 miles to the north.

G1. Only launch control center on a college campus. Western Nebraska Community College, formerly the Sioux Ordnance Depot, manufacturing munitions in World War II and the Korean War, offers courses ranging from diesel mechanics to cosmetology.

H10. On January 10, 1984, an Air Force emergency response team parked an armored vehicle on the lid of this silo in a last-ditch effort to prevent what appeared to be the launch of its malfunctioning missile. The problem proved later to be in the monitoring system at the nearby launch control center rather than in the missile itself.

The incident, unreported at the time, was discovered almost four years after the fact by investigative reporter Katharine Collins of the *Casper (WY) Star-Tribune.*

Capt. Bill Kalton, deputy chief of public affairs at F. E. Warren Air Force Base, explained that if the silo lid had opened, prior to a launch, the armored vehicle would have fallen into the silo, damaging the missile and blocking its path.

J3. Annual Good Friday worship services held here under the leadership of the Rev. Ed Bigler, pastor of the United Methodist Church in nearby Peetz from 1983 to 1988. The position of the United Methodist Church nationally is that "the production, possession, or use of nuclear weapons be condemned."

J8. Scene of an overnight vigil and Easter sunrise service April 3, 1988. About a dozen took part.

Q2. Used by the Air Force and Boeing Corporation as a training site for installation of MX missiles in Minuteman silos. Peace activists monitoring MX installation used it as an observation base in the last week of August, 1986.

North Dakota

In some ways North Dakota is like all of America. It's a land-based territory of plowshares and swords, giant combines and huge ICBMs, with resources to feed the world or destroy it. But it's more obvious here.

—Syndicated columnist Ellen Goodman, April 1983.

Missile silo I3, near Stanley, North Dakota.

© John Hooton

Editor's note: There are two Minuteman missile silo fields in North Dakota. Following are the directions for the Minot silo field. Directions for the silos in the Grand Forks field follow the Grand Forks map on page 45. Photo portrait of the Grand Forks field is on page 95.

FLIGHT A

A1. Strip Mine launch center. From Balfour, go northwest 2.7 miles on U.S. 52, then right .2 mile. Control center is on the right.

A2. Meadowlark Song missile. From Balfour, go southeast 4.1 miles on U.S. 52, then left 5.2 miles on State Highway 14. Missile is on the right.

A3. Duck missile. From Drake go north .5 mile. Missile is on the right.

A4. Auschwitz missile. From Balfour, go southeast 2.5 miles on U.S. 52. Missile is on the right.

A5. Sigmund missile. From Drake, go northwest 2.8 miles on U.S. 52, then left 3.3 miles. Missile is on the left.

A6. Cossack missile. From the railroad tracks at Kief, go south 1.2 miles on State Highway 53, then continue straight on a gravel road .2 mile, then left .2 mile. Missile is on the left.

A7. High Tech missile. From the railroad tracks at Kief, go north .5 mile on State Highway 53, then left 3 miles, then right 2.1 miles. Missile is on the right.

A8. Dogden missile. From the northeast corner of Butte, go north .6 mile. Missile is on the right.

A9. Viking missile. From Bergen, go southeast 2 miles on U.S. 52, then left 1.2 miles. Missile is on the left.

A10. Blitzkrieg missile. From Karlsruhe, go north .8 mile. Missile is on the left.

A11. Guarded missile. From Karlsruhe, go south 3.8 miles, then left 1.7 miles. Missile is on the right.

FLIGHT B

B1. Menno Simons Nemesis launch center. From Velva, go south 9.7 miles on State Highway 41. Control center is on the left.

B2. Bulimia missile. From U.S. 52 at Voltaire, go north 3.9 miles. Missile is on the right.

B3. Dorman Dachau missile. From the junction of State Highway 41 and Central Avenue East at Velva, go east 9.5 miles on the road to Karlsruhe, then left 4 miles. Missile is on the left.

B4. Voltaire's Volley missile. From Voltaire, go east 1 mile on U.S. 52, then right 1.7 miles. Missile is on the left.

B5. America's Folly missile. From Voltaire, go east 1 mile on U.S. 52, then right 6 miles. Missile is on the left.

B6. Sleeping Auschwitz missile. From the railroad tracks at Kongsberg, go north .6 mile on County Road 27. Missile is on the right.

B7. Backlash missile. From Ruso go south .4 mile on State Highway 41. Missile is on the left.

B8. Benedict's Boomerang missile. From Benedict, go north 4.7 miles on County Road 23. Missile is on the left.

B9. Treblinka Tremor missile. From Benedict, go north 8.8 miles on County Road 23, then right .2 mile. Missile is on the left.

B10. Boondock missile. From Velva, go south 4 miles on State Highway 41, then right 2 miles, then left 1 mile, then right .4 mile. Missile is on the right.

B11. No-Go missile. From Velva, go south 1 mile on State Highway 41. Missile is on the right.

FLIGHT C

C1. Out of Control launch control center. From the first intersection with State Highway 53 south of Ruso, go south 8.3 miles on State Highway 41, then right 5 miles on County Road 6, then left .2 mile. Control center is on the left.

C2. Ruso's Rue missile. From the first intersection with State Highway 53 south of Ruso, go south 5.8 miles on State Highway 41. Missile is on the right.

C3. Dogden Demise missile. From Ruso go east 6.2 miles on State Highway 53 to County Road 27, then right 3.1 miles. Missile is on the right.

C4. Mother Russo missile. From Turtle Lake, go north 11.4 miles on State Highway 41. Missile is on the right.

C5. Crane Shooter missile. From Turtle Lake, go north 6 miles on State Highway 41 to County Road 10, then right 1.6 miles. Missile is on the left.

C6. Fallen Elm missile. From Turtle Lake, go north 8 miles on State Highway 41, then left 3 miles on County Road 8. Missile is on the right.

C7. Myrtle Mae Menace missile. From State Highway 53 east of Benedict, go south 15.6 miles on County Road 23. Missile is on the left.

C8. Ned the Nuke missile. From State Highway 53 east of Benedict, go south 11.1 miles on County Road 23. Missile is on the left.

C9. Earth Cancer missile. From State Highway 53 east of Benedict, go south 9 miles on County Road 23, then right 4 miles, then right 1 mile. Missile is on the right.

C10. Lie Low Mile missile. From State Highway 53 east of Benedict, go south 4.3 miles on County Road 23. Missile is on the left.

C11. Big Bump missile. From the junction of State Highway 53 and the road to Benedict, go east 2.4 miles on State Highway 53. Missile is on the right.

FLIGHT D

D1. Death From Max launch control center. From Max, go south 2 miles on U.S. 83. Control center is on the right.

D2. Max Mutant Machine missile. From Max, go north 6.5 miles on U.S. 83. Missile is on the left.

D3. Max Syndrome missile. From Max, go north 3.6 miles on U.S. 83, then right 3.9 miles on County Road

On Cheyenne land

Twelve missiles and one launch control center administered by Minot Air Force Base are on the Fort Berthold Reservation of the Cheyenne Nation. The missile silos are E8, E9, E10, F7, F8, F9, H4, H5, H6, H7, H8 and H9. The launch control center is H1.

24, then right .2 mile. Missile is on the right.

D4. Bluddlefilth missile. From Max, go south 3.4 miles on U.S. 83, then left 4.7 miles on County Road 4. Missile is on the left.

D5. Death Tongue missile. From Garrison, go east on State Highway 37 to U.S. 83, then north 1.3 miles. Missile is on the right.

D6. Dr. Doom missile. From Garrison, go east on State Highway 37 to U.S. 83, then north 5.8 miles. Missile is on the right.

D7. Gross Wrecking missile. From State Highway 37 at Garrison, go north 1 mile on County Road 15, following Soo Line Avenue left, then go right 1.2 miles on a gravel road. Missile is on the left.

D8. Blind Lie missile. From State Highway 37 at Garrison, go north 6 miles on County Road 15, following Soo Line Avenue left. Missile is on the right.

D9. Mound of Mourning missile. From U.S. 83 north of Max, go west 5.8 miles on State Highway 53, then left 4.8 miles on County Road 15, crossing railroad tracks. Missile is on the left.

D10. Mind Tailings missile. From Douglas, go east 1.8 miles on State Highway 53. Missile is on the right.

D11. The Cover Up missile. From U.S. 83 north of Max, go west 2.6 miles on State Highway 53. Missile is on the right.

FLIGHT E

E1. Pentagon's Pride launch control center. From Roseglen, go east 7 miles on State Highway 37, then left .3 mile on State Highway 28. Control center is on the right.

E2. Six-Six-Six missile. From Douglas, go south 3.5 miles, then right .7 mile. Missile is on the left.

E3. Los Alamos missile. From Garrison, go west 5.3 miles on State Highway 37, then right 3 miles on County Road 13. Where County Road 13 veers right, continue forward 2.1 miles on County Road 6, then right .4 mile. Missile is on the left.

E4. Livermore missile. From Garrison, go west 3.7 miles on State High-

way 37. Missile is on the right.

E5. The Horror! The Horror! missile. From Garrison, go west 8.7 miles on State Highway 37. Missile is on the right.

E6. Shiver Me Timbers missile. From Roseglen, go east 7 miles on State Highway 37, then right 4 miles on State Highway 28. Missile is on the right.

E7. Deadly Gopher missile. From Roseglen, go east 1.4 miles on State Highway 37, then right 7 miles on County Road 9, then left 1.9 miles. Missile is on the right.

E8. Last Laugh missile. From Roseglen, go east 1.4 miles on State Highway 37, then right 3.9 miles on County Road 9, then right 1.5 miles. Missile is on the left.

E9. IMU-2 missile. From Roseglen, go east 1.4 miles on State Highway 37, then right 3.9 miles on County Road 9, then right 6 miles. Missile is on the right.

E10. Insane E missile. From Roseglen, go west 2.1 miles on State Highway 37. Missile is on the right.

E11. Bleakheaded Booby missile. From Roseglen, go east 1.4 miles on State Highway 37, then left 3 miles. Missile is on the right.

FLIGHT F

F1. Ryder Fox launch control center. From Ryder, go south 1 mile on State Highway 28. Control center is on the left.

F2. Flyboys' missile. From Ryder, go north 3.1 miles on State Highway 28. Missile is on the right.

F3. Foolhardy missile. From Ryder, go north 4 miles on State Highway 28, then right 4.7 miles on State Highway 23. Missile is on the left.

F4. Stinky Slough missile. From Douglas, go north 4.1 miles on County Road 13, then left .6 mile on County Road 22. Missile is on the right.

F5. Devil's Den missile. From Douglas, go west 3.6 miles on State Highway 53. Missile is on the left.

F6. Mudhole missile. From Ryder, go south 4 miles on State Highway 28, then right 3.8 miles. Missile is on the left.

Three-phase transformers over nuclear missile silos help identify them from afar.

Bonnie Urfer

F7. Vulcan missile. From Roseglen, go east 1.4 miles on State Highway 37, then left 6 miles on County Road 9, then left 3.3 miles. Missile is on the right.

F8. Bad Joke missile. From Makoti, go south 2.6 miles on County Road 9, then right 6.9 miles, then left 2 miles, then left .5 mile. Missile is on the left.

F9. Plowshares missile. From Makoti, go south 2.6 miles on County Road 9, then right 1.7 miles. Missile is on the left.

F10. Children at Risk missile. From Makoti, go north 1 mile, then left 4.1 miles on State Highway 23. Missile is on the right.

F11. Makoti Lodge missile. From Makoti, go north 1 mile, then right .7 mile on State Highway 23. Missile is on the right.

FLIGHT G

G1. The Little Shop of Horrors launch control center. From the west end of Plaza, go north 6.8 miles. Control center is on the right.

G2. The Hottest Place in Hell missile. From the west end of Plaza, go north 11 miles, then right 1 mile. Missile is on the left.

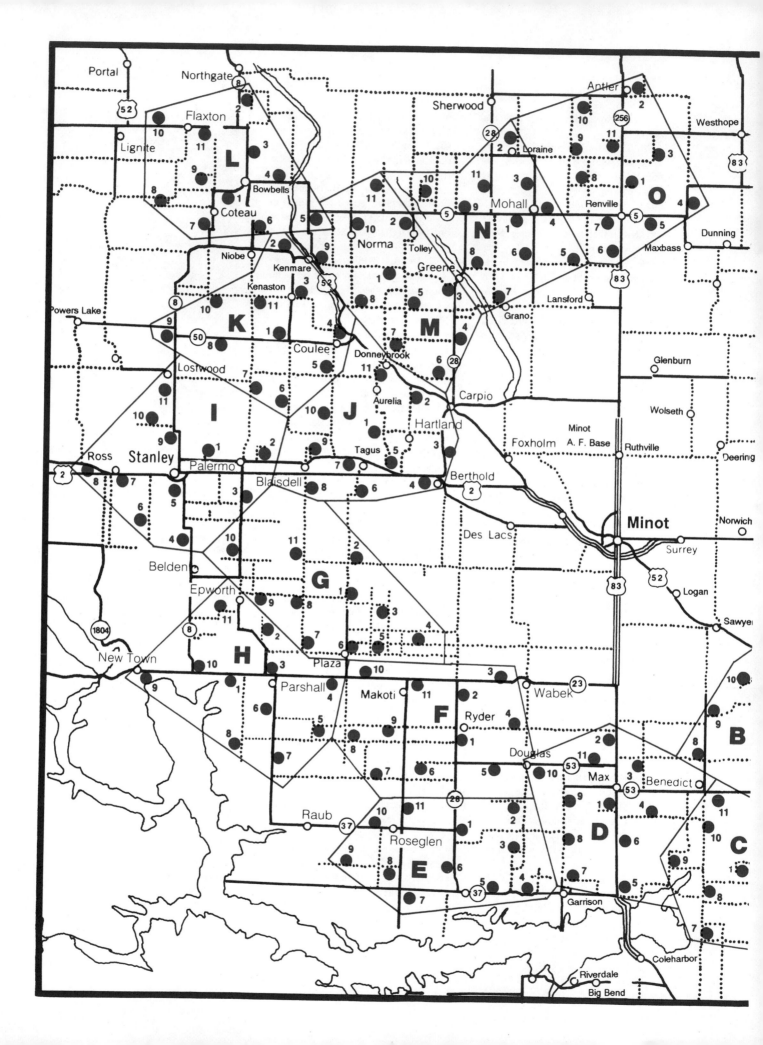

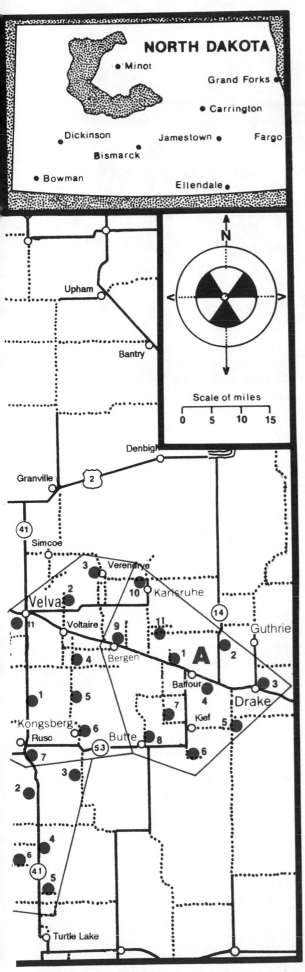

G3. The Living End missile. From State Highway 23, go north 3 miles toward Plaza, then right 3.3 miles on County Road 18, then left 4 miles to the Spring Valley Church, then right 1 mile, then left 3.5 miles. Missile is on the left.

G4. Yet to Be Determined missile. From State Highway 23, go north 3 miles toward Plaza, then right 8 miles on County Road 18, then left 1.9 miles on County Road 9, then right 2.4 miles. Missile is on the left.

G5. Sweet Clover missile. From State Highway 23 go north 3 miles toward Plaza, then right 3.3 miles on County Road 18, then left 2 miles, then right 1 mile. Missile is on the right.

G6. Mysterious missile. From the west edge of Plaza, go north 1.1 miles. Missile is on the right.

G7. Queen of Sheba missile. From Plaza, go west 5 miles, then right 2.2 miles. Missile is on the right.

G8. Creeping Jenny missile. From the west end of Plaza, go north 7 miles, then left 5 miles, then left .1 mile. Missile is on the right.

G9. Mourning missile. From Belden, go east 7.8 miles on a paved road that turns to gravel, then right 1 mile, then left .1 mile. Missile is on the right.

G10. Canada Thistle missile. From Belden, go east 5.8 miles on a paved road that turns to gravel, then left 3.3 miles. Missile is on the left.

G11. Wild Sunflowers missile. From the west end of Plaza, go north 7 miles, then left 5 miles, then right 5 miles. Missile is on the left.

FLIGHT H

H1. Hotel Hell launch control center. From the junction of State Highways 23 and 37, go west 4.2 miles on State Highway 23. Control center is on the left.

H2. The Hive missile. From the junction of State Highways 23 and 37, go north 3 miles on State Highway 37 to a "T", then left 1.3 miles, then right 3 miles. Missile is on the right.

H3. Right Wing missile. From the junction of State Highways 23 and 37, go north 1 mile on State Highway 37.

Missile is on the right.

H4. Sod Buster missile. From the junction of State Highways 23 and 37, go east 6 miles on State Highway 23. Missile is on the right.

H5. Piggy missile. From the junction of State Highways 23 and 37, go south 4.9 miles on State Highway 37, then left 4 miles, then right 1 mile, then left .1 mile. Missile is on the right.

H6. Garbage missile. From the junction of State Highways 23 and 37, go south 3.7 miles on State Highway 37. Missile is on the right.

H7. Mourning Cloak missile. From the junction of State Highways 23 and 37, go south 8.5 miles on State Highway 37. Missile is on the left.

H8. Behind the Eight Ball missile. From the junction of State Highways 23 and 37, go south 5.8 miles on State Highway 37, then right 4 miles, then left .1 mile. Missile is on the right.

H9. New Town's Nuke missile. From New Town, go east 2 miles on State Highway 23. Missile is on the right.

H10. Sakajawea's Sorrow missile. From the junction of State Highways 8 and 23, go .1 mile north on State Highway 8. Missile is on the right.

H11. Little Boy's Baby missile. From the junction of State Highways 8 and 23, go north 7.3 miles on State Highway 8, then right. After 3 miles the road jogs left 1 mile, then right .5 mile. Missile is on the left.

FLIGHT I

I1. Northern Harrier launch control center. From Palermo, go west 3.8 miles on Old U.S. 2, then right .2 mile. Control center is at the end of the road.

I2. Meadowlark missile. From Palermo, go east 2 miles on Old U.S. 2, then left 2.1 miles, then right .2 mile. Missile is on the right.

I3. Gull missile. From U.S. 2 at the Palermo exit, go south 3.7 miles. Missile is on the left.

I4. Little Knife River missile. From Belden, go north 3.7 miles on State Highway 8. Missile is on the left.

I5. Killdeer missile. From U.S. 2 at Stanley, go south 1.8 miles on State Highway 8. Missile is on the right.

I6. Pronghorn missile. From State Highway 8 at Stanley, go west 4 miles on U.S. 2, then left 5.5 miles. Missile is on the right.

I7. Prairie Rose missile. From Ross, go east 2 miles on U.S. 2. Missile is on the right.

I8. Shoveler missile. From Ross, go west .7 mile on U.S. 2, then right 2 miles on Old U.S. 2 (west). Missile is on the left.

I9. Skunk missile. From the junction of Old U.S. 2 and State Highway 8 north of Stanley, go north 4 miles on State Highway 8. Missile is on the left.

I10. Hungarian Gray Partridge missile. From the junction of Old U.S. 2 and State Highway 8 north of Stanley, go north 6.2 miles on State Highway 8, then left 2.5 miles. Missile is on the right.

I11. Lostwood missile. From the junction of Old U.S. 2 and State Highway 8 north of Stanley, go north 9 miles on State Highway 8. Missile is on the left.

FLIGHT J

J1. Peace Garden State launch control center. From the junction of U.S. 2 and State Highway 28, go west 4.3 miles on U.S. 2, then right 3 miles on County Road 5W (Old U.S. 2), then right 2.8 miles (continuing forward). Control center is on the left.

J2. Bill Langer's missile. From Donnybrook, go southeast 3.5 miles on U.S. 52, then right 1.9 miles on County Road 5. Missile is on the left.

J3. Berthold's Folly missile. From U.S. 2 at Berthold, go north 4.9 miles on State Highway 28. Missile is on the right.

J4. Hang Head missile. From State Highway 28 at Berthold, go west 2.2 miles on U.S. 2. Missile is on the left.

J5. Shame on North Dakota missile. From the junction of U.S. 2 and State Highway 28, go west 4.3 miles on U.S. 2, then right 3 miles on County Road 5W (Old U.S. 2), then right .1 mile. Missile is on the right.

J6. Meadowlark Serenade missile. From U.S. 2 at Tagus exit, go south 2.6 miles. Missile is on the left.

J7. How Did you Get Here? mis-

sile. From Tagus, go north .3 mile to old U.S. 2, then left 2 miles. Missile is on the left.

J8. We'll Help You Leave missile. From U.S. 2, at Blaisdell exit, go south 2.5 miles. Missile is on the left.

J9. Leave This Land For the Prairie Dogs and Wildflowers missile. From Blaisdell, go east .2 mile on Old U.S. 2, then left 1.2 miles. Missile is on the right.

J10. Missing from 4H Neighborhood Roster missile. From Tagus, go north .3 mile to Old U.S. 2, then left 3.6 miles, then right 4.5 miles. Missile is on the left.

J11. Beast and the Beauty missile. From Donnybrook, go southwest 2 miles on County Road 5. Missile is on the left.

FLIGHT K

K1. Nebuchadnezzar launch control center. From Coulee, go west 4.8 miles on State Highway 50. Control center is on the right.

K2. Emm missile. From U.S. 52 at Kenmare, go west 1 mile , then right 2 miles on County Road 2. Missile is on the right.

K3. Sorry missile. From U.S. 52 at Kenmare, go west 1 mile on County Road 2, then straight 5 miles to

Peace school at silo E46 near Starkweather, North Dakota; Air Force vehicles stand guard inside the fence.

Grand Forks Herald photo by John Stennes

County Road 4, then left .8 mile. Missile is on the left.

K4. Xerxes missile. From Coulee, go north .8 mile. Missile is on the right.

K5. Herodias missile. From Coulee, go south 4 miles. Missile is on the right.

K6. Sennacherib missile. From Coulee, go west 4 miles on State Highway 50, then left 8 miles. Missile is on the right.

K7. Sargon missile. From Coulee, go west 9 miles on State Highway 50, then left 5.6 miles. Missile is on the left.

K8. Tiglath-Pileser missile. From Coulee, go west 12 miles on State Highway 50. Missile is on the left.

K9. Dog's Life missile. From the southern junction of State Highways 8 and 50, go south .1 mile on State Highway 8. Missile is on the right.

K10. Brian Mulroney missile. From U.S. 52 at Kenmare, go west 1 mile on County Road 2, then straight 5 miles to County Road 4 outside Kenaston, then right 7.8 miles. Missile is on the left.

K11. Little Red School House missile. From U.S. 2 at Kenmare, go west 1 mile on County Road 2, then straight 5 miles to County Road 4 outside

Kenaston, then right 3.8 miles. Missile is on the left.

FLIGHT L

L1. Key To Pieces launch control center. From Bowbells, go southwest 1.2 miles on State Highway 8. Control center is on the left.

L2. Ring Around the Rosie missile. From Northgate, go south 2.6 miles on State Highway 8, then left 1 mile, then right 1.5 miles. Missile is on the right.

L3. "Skeksis" missile. From Bowbells, go north 3.5 miles on U.S. 52/State Highway 8. Missile is on the right.

L4. Drop Bye-Bye missile. From Bowbells, go east 3.5 miles on U.S. 52. Missile is on the left.

L5. Horse Plop Drop missile. From County Road 2 at Kenmare, go north 6.2 miles on U.S. 52, then right .6 mile on State Highway 5. Missile is on the right.

L6. River Styx missile. From Bowbells, go south 5.1 miles on County Road 17, then left .6 mile. Missile is on the left.

L7. Triumph missile. From Bowbells, go southwest 8.7 miles on State Highway 8. Missile is on the right.

L8. Foul Whistle missile. From Bowbells, go southwest 7 miles on State Highway 8, then right 5 miles on County Road 12, then right .8 mile. Missile is on the left.

What's inside the fence. Top: underground view of a Minuteman missile silo; Center: the silo lid and surrounding surface area; Bottom: cutaway view of a launch control center and its underground capsule.

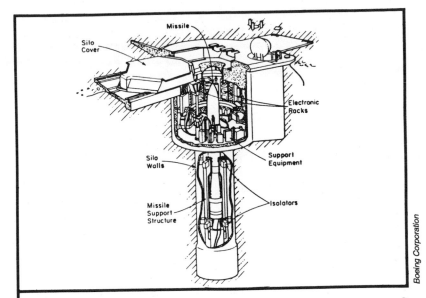

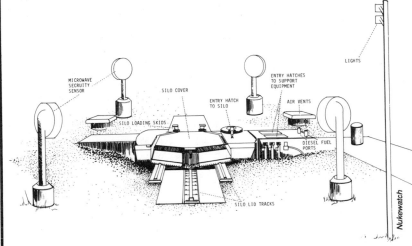

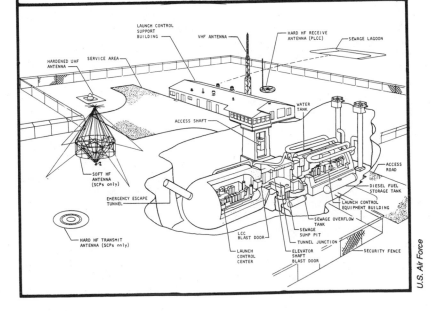

L9. Diamond Bullet missile. From Bowbells, go southwest 4.9 miles on State Highway 8, then right .1 mile on County Road 15, then right 2 miles, then left 1.8 miles. Missile is on the left.

L10. Flight to Hades missile. From the railroad underpass south of Flaxton, go west 2.3 miles on U.S. 52. Missile is on the right.

L11. "Moloch" missile. From the railroad underpass south of Flaxton, go east 2.5 miles on U.S. 52. Missile is on the right.

FLIGHT M

M1. The Secret launch control center. From the railroad tracks in Norma, go south 3.7 miles on County Road 1, which becomes County Road 3, then left 4.5 miles on County Road 2. Control center is on the right.

M2. Thistle missile. From the railroad tracks in Tolley, go north 1.3 miles on County Road 3. Missile is on the left.

M3. Atlas Shrugged missile. From the railroad tracks in Greene, go southwest .8 mile on State Highway 28. Missile is on the right.

M4. Destination-Termination missile. From the railroad tracks in Greene, go southwest 5.7 miles on State Highway 28. Missile is on the left.

M5. Greene Glass missile. From the railroad tracks in Green, go southwest 3.1 miles on State Highway 28, then right 5 miles on County Road 16. Missile is on the right.

M6. Prairie Primeval missile. From Carpio, go north 4 miles on State Highway 28, then left 1.3 miles. Missile is on the right.

M7. Star Wars Stiletto missile. From U.S. 52 at Donnybrook, go north 1.8 miles on County Road 5, then right 1.6 miles on County Road 7, following the road another 1.3 miles after it turns left. Missile is on the left.

M8. Grapes of Wrath missile. From the junction of State Highway 50 and U.S. 52 at Coulee, go north 5.2 miles on U.S. 52, then right 2.3 miles. Missile is on the left.

M9. Fright-Mare missile. From U.S. 52 at Kenmare, go east 2.7 miles on County Road 2. Missile is on the left.

M10. Top Gum missile. From the railroad tracks in Norma, go north 1.5 miles on County Road 1. Missile is on the right.

M11. Pleasant Fairy of Peace missile. From the railroad tracks in Tolley, go north 2.7 miles on County Road 3, then left 3.8 miles on State Highway 5, then right 3 miles. Missile is on the left.

FLIGHT N

N1. Slo Mo launch control center. From County Road 9 in Mohall, go west 3.3 miles on State Highway 5. Control center is on the left.

N2. Fear Monger's Shop missile. From Loraine, go east .4 mile, then left 1.7 miles. Missile is on the left.

N3. Blasphemy missile. From State Highway 5 at Mohall, go north 4.3 miles on County Road 9. Missile is on the left.

N4. Justice Stops Here missile. From the county courthouse in Mohall, go east 1.7 miles. Missile is on the left.

N5. Warning Sign missile. From Renville, go west 3.9 miles on State Highway 5, then left 4.9 miles, then right 1.1 miles. Missile is on the right.

N6. Mohall Horror-Hall missile. From State Highway 5 at Mohall, go south 4.1 miles on County Road 9. Missile is on the right.

N7. Whamo Grano Blamo missile. From Grano, go west .8 mile on County Road 16, then right .5 mile. Missile is on the right.

N8. Holy Terror missile. From the railroad tracks at Greene, go north 2.5 miles on State Highway 28, then right 2.7 miles. Missile is on the left.

N9. "To Be or Not to Be" missile. From County Road 9 at Mohall, go west 8.5 miles on State Highway 5. Missile is on the right.

N10. Mudhole missile. From County Road 9 at Mohall, go west 9.8 miles on State Highway 5, then right 1.9 miles on Mouse River Road, then left 2.1 miles, then right 1.5 miles. Missile is on the right.

N11. Okey-Dokey missile. From County Road 9 at Mohall, go west 4.9 miles on State Highway 5, then right 4.3 miles on State Highway 28. Missile is on the left.

FLIGHT 0

O1. Death Camp launch control center. From Renville, go north 4 miles on State Highway 256, then right .6 mile. Control center is on the left.

O2. King Stag missile. From Antler, go south .4 mile, then left 1 mile, then left .5 mile. Missile is on the left.

O3. Westhope's Despair missile. From U.S. 83 in Westhope, go west 8.8 miles, then left 2.5 miles. Missile is on the left.

O4. Twisted Sister missile. From Renville, go east 8.8 miles on U.S. 83/State Highway 5. Missile is on the right.

O5. Oil Can Harry missile. From Renville, go east 2.8 miles. Missile is on the right.

O6. Dick Dastardly missile. From Renville, go south 4.4 miles on U.S. 83. Missile is on the right.

O7. Cow Pucky missile. From Renville, go west 2.1 miles on State Highway 5. Missile is on the left.

O8. Silent Farms missile. From Renville, go north 4 miles on State Highway 256, then left 4 miles, then right .2 mile. Missile is on the left.

O9. Empty Schoolhouse missile. From Renville, go north 7 miles on State Highway 256, then left 6 miles, then right 1.9 miles. Missile is on the right.

O10. Mushroom Farm missile. From Antler, go south .4 mile, then right 3.7 miles (crossing State Route 256), then left 1.2 miles. Missile is on the right.

O11. Endless Night missile. From Renville, go north 8.8 miles on State Highway 256, then left .2 mile. Missile is on the left.

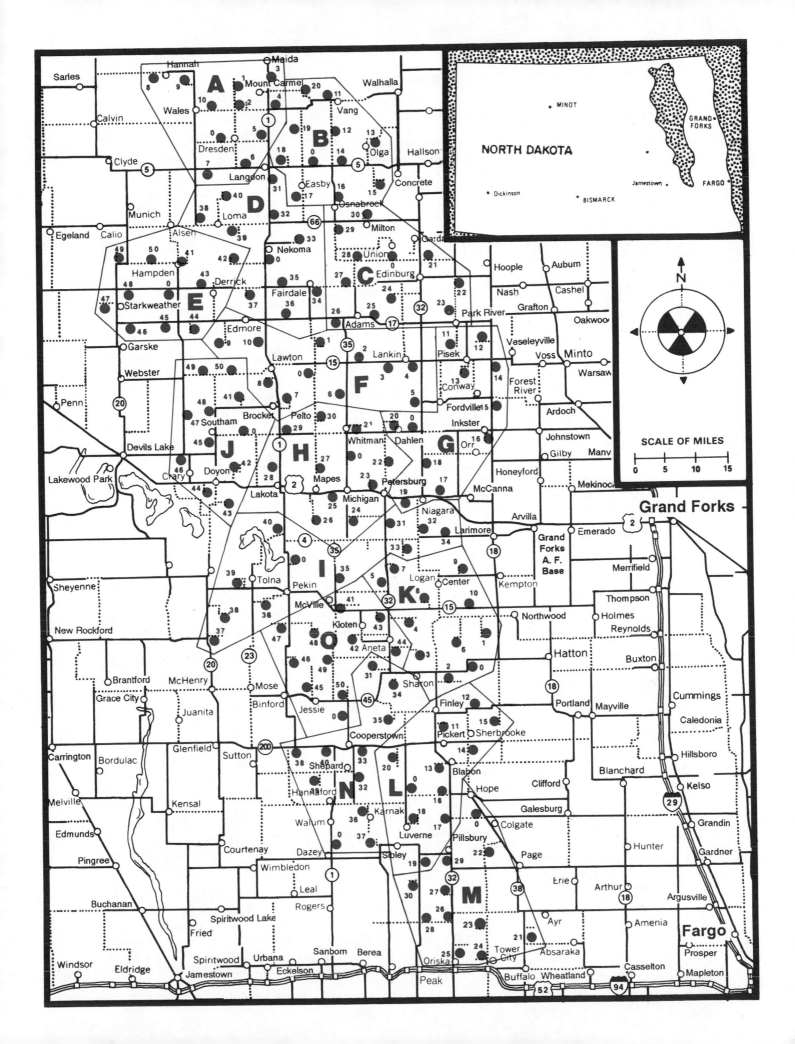

FLIGHT A

A0. Criminal Intent launch control center. From Dresden, go .5 mile southwest, then right 1.2 miles. Control center is on the right.

A1. Pierre Trudeau's missile. From Dresden, go 9.5 miles north. Missile is on the right.

A2. Physicist's Dream missile. From Dresden, go 4.5 miles north, then right 2 miles, then left .5 mile. Missile is on the left.

A3. Maple Leaf missile. From State Highway 5 in Langdon, go north 14.2 miles on State Highway 1. Missile is on the right.

A4. Leo Laukki missile. From State Highway 5 in Langdon, go north 9 miles on State Highway 1, then right 1.5 miles. Missile is on the left.

A5. Selma Jokela McCone missile. From State Highway 5 in Langdon, go north 4.8 miles on State Highway 1. Missile is on the left.

A6. Good Riddance missile. From State Highway 1 in Langdon, go west 3.5 miles on State Highway 5. Missile is on the right.

A7. Taavi Taino missile. From State Highway 1 in Langdon, go west 9 miles on State Highway 5. Missile is on the left.

A8. Knows No Boundaries missile. From Hannah, go west 1.5 miles. Missile is on the left.

A9. Helmi Mattson missile. From Wales, go north 3.8 miles, then left .3 mile. Missile is on the right.

A10. Babylon Falling Down missile. From Wales, go east 2.5 miles on a gravel road. Missile is on the left.

FLIGHT B

B0. Tax Payers' launch control center. From Langdon, go east 7.5 miles on State Highway 5. Control center is on the left.

B11. Frost-Fire missile. From Vang, go west .5 mile. Missile is on the right.

B12. Rude missile. From Langdon, go east 10 miles on State Highway 5, then left 5 miles on a gravel road. Missile is on the right.

B13. Damage Done missile. From Olga, go north 1.4 miles, then right 1.4

miles on gravel roads. Missile is on the right.

B14. Anniversary Rock missile. From Langdon, go east 12.5 miles on State Highway 5. Missile is on the left.

B15. Time Bomb missile. From Olga, go south 3 miles to State Highway 5, then left .5 mile, then right (on Senator Young Dam Road) 2.9 miles, then left 1.5 miles. Missile is on the right.

B16. Puck's Breath missile. From Osnabrock, go north 2 miles. Missile is on the right.

B17. The Big Lie missile. From Easby, go south 2 miles. Missile is on the right.

B18. Wild Thistle missile. From Langdon, go east 3 miles on State Highway 5, then left 1 mile. Missile is on the left.

B19. Potato Bud missile. From Langdon, go east 5 miles on State Highway 5, then left 5.5 miles. Missile is on the left.

B20. Bitter-Root missile. From Mount Carmel, go east 1.1 miles, then left .3 mile on State Highway 1, then right 5.2 miles. At an intersection, go left 1 mile, then right .2 mile. Missile is on the right.

FLIGHT C

C0. Heart of Darkness launch control center. From Edinburg, go north 3.4 miles on State Highway 32, then left 4.8 miles on County Road 1. Control center is on the right.

C21. Agassiz's Agony missile. From Edinburg, go north 3.4 miles on State Highway 32, then right 1.4 miles on County Road 1. Missile is on the left.

C22. Prairie Kali missile. From Edinburg, go east 6 miles on County Road 9, then right .5 mile on a gravel road. Missile is on the left.

C23. Kissinger's Remorse missile. From State Highway 17 in Park River, go north 2 miles on County Road 12. Missile is on the left.

C24. Naked Lunch missile. From State Highway 32 in Edinburg, go south 2 miles on County Road 9, then right (past cemetery) 4.5 miles. Missile is on the left.

C25. Mr. Kurtz missile. From

County Road 16 in Adams, go east 3 miles on State Highway 17. Missile is on the left.

C26. Flower of Evil missile. From the junction of State Highways 17 and 35 west of Adams, go west .1 mile on State Highway 17. Missile is on the left.

C27. Ghost Dance missile. From Fairdale, go east 6.2 miles on County Road 9. Missile is on the left.

C28. Voices Catching Up missile. From Adams, go north 8.5 miles on County Road 16, then right .5 mile on County Road 1. Missile is on the left.

C29. Paradise Lost missile. From Osnabrock, go south to State Highway 66, then continue south 1.5 miles on a paved road. Missile is on the left.

C30. Mim's Roots missile. From the Milton turn-off on State Highway 66, go north 2 miles on a narrow, curving road. Missile is on the right

FLIGHT D

D0. Every Day's Fear launch control center. From Nekoma, go south 1.4 miles on State Highway 1. Control center is on the left.

D31. Just War missile. From State Highway 5 in Langdon, go south 3.7 miles on State Highway 1. Missile is on the left.

D32. A.B. Makela missile. From State Highway 5 in Langdon, go south 8.8 miles on State Highway 1. Missile is on the left.

D33. Scoundrel's Last Refuge missile. From Nekoma, go north 1.1 miles on State Highway 1, then right 5 miles on a road that is first paved then gravel, then .7 mile left on a gravel road. Missile is on the right.

D34. Temporary Madness missile. From Fairdale, go east 1 mile on County Road 9. Missile is on the right.

D35. Reality of Power missile. From Fairdale, go west 4.2 miles on Country Road 9. Missile is on the right.

D36. Antero Tanner missile. From the junction of State Highways 17 and 1, go east 3.6 miles on State Highway 17. Missile is on the left.

D37. Gravy Sucking missile. From the junction of State Highway 1 and County Road 9 (the road to Fairdale),

Surveillance sensors stand like sentinels on the western range.

go west 3 miles on County Road 9, then left .7 mile on a gravel road. Missile is on the left.

D38. Blind Patriotism missile. From Loma, go west 3.3 miles on State Highway 66, then right .2 mile on a gravel road. Missile is on the right.

D39. Prairie Ransom missile. From Loma, go east 3 miles on State Highway 66, then right .8 mile. Missile is on the right.

D40. Martin Hendrickson missile. From Loma, go left 4 miles on a gravel road, then right 1 mile, then left .2 mile. Missile is on the right.

FLIGHT E

E0. Chains of Command launch control center. From Hampden, go south 4.3 miles on County Road 3, then right 1.4 miles on County Road 9. Control center is on the left.

E41. Burning Earth missile. From Hampden, go east .5 mile, then left 1.5 miles on County Road 3. Missile is on the left.

E42. Broken Promise missile. From Nekoma, go south 2 miles on State Highway 1, then right 6.4 miles (to a crossroad), then right .4 mile. Missile is on the right.

E43. Trail of Tears missile. From the junction of State Highway 1 and County Road 9 (The road to Fairdale),

go west 9.5 miles on County Road 9. Missile is on the right.

E44. Poison Payload missile. From Edmore, go west 8 miles on State Highway 17, then left .3 mile. Missile is on the left.

E45. Jackboot missile. From Edmore, go west 12.6 miles on State Highway 17. Missile is on the left.

E46. Peace School missile. From Starkweather, go south 3.3 miles on State Highway 20, then left 2.5 miles on State Highway 17. Missile is on the right.

E47. Banal missile. From Starkweather, go north .3 mile on State Highway 17/20, then left 2.4 miles. Missile is on the left.

E48. Hide the Sun missile. From Starkweather, go north 2.3 miles on State Highway 20, then right 2.7 miles on County Road 9. Missile is on the right.

E49. Alone with Fear missile. From Starkweather, go north 6.1 miles on State Highway 20 to the point where the road curves to the east, then continue north 1 mile. Missile is on the right.

E50. Machine Money missile. From Hampden, go west .6 mile on County Road 3. Where Road 3 curves south, take a gravel road north .3 mile, then go left 4.4 miles. Missile is on the right.

FLIGHT F

F0. Forbidden Orders launch control center. From Lawton, go east 6.7 miles on County Road 15, then right 1.4 miles on County Road 22. Control center is on the right.

F1. Planetary Slaughterhouse missile. From Lawton, go east 6.7 miles on County Road 15, then left 3.9 miles on County Road 22, then right .2 mile on County Road 22A. Missile is on the left.

F2. Disarming D. Fields missile. From Lankin, go west 7.6 miles on County Road 15. Missile is on the right.

F3. Nuclear Winter missile. From Lankin, go west 3 miles on County Road 15. Missile is on the right.

F4. Dakota's Denial missile. From Lankin, go east 2 miles on County Road 15. Missile is on the right.

F5. Fearful Folly missile. From Fordville, go west 3 miles to State Highway 32. Missile is on west side of Highway 32.

F6. Forest River missile. From Lankin, go west 9 miles on County Road 15, then left 4.5 miles on State Highway 35. Missile is on the right.

F7. Brocket's Rocket missile. From Brocket, just south of junction of State Highway 1 and County Road 7, go east 2.2 miles (past cemetery),

Between classes in a North Dakota wheat field.

Edith Sears

then left 1 mile, then left .4 mile. Missile is on the right.

F8. Megadeath missile. From Lawton, go south 1.4 miles on State Highway 1, then right .8 mile. Missile is on the left.

F9. Nuclear Wheat missile. From Edmore, go west 3 miles on State Highway 17, then left 3.8 miles on County Road 4. Missile is on the right.

F10. The End missile. From Lawton, go north 4.5 miles on State Highway 1. Missile is on the left.

FLIGHT G

G0. Karma launch control center. From U.S. 2, go north 9.9 miles on State Highway 32, then left .3 mile on County Road 1. Control center is on the right.

G11. Spirit of Poison missile. From State Highway 17 in Park River, go south 2 miles on County Road 12-B, then continue south 1.6 miles. Missile is on the right.

G12. Prairie Puzzle missile. From Park River, go east 5 miles on State Highway 17, then right 3.2 miles on State Highway 18, then right 1.1 miles. Missile is on the right.

G13. Farm Crisis missile. From Pisek, go south 1 mile on County Road 12A, then right 1.1 miles, then left 1.1 miles. Missile is on the left.

G14. Breadbasket missile. From Pisek, go east 4 miles on County Road 15, then right 1.5 miles on State Highway 18. Missile is on the left.

G15. Soo Line missile. From Inkster, go east 1 mile to State Highway 18, then left 4.5 miles on Highway 18. Missile is on the right.

G16. Blackout missile. From Inkster, go south 1.3 miles. Missile is on the left.

G17 Turtle River missile. From the intersection of U.S. 2 and State Highway 32 (at Niagara), go east 1.9 miles on U.S. 2, then leave U.S. 2 and continue east .7 mile on County Road 11. Missile is on the left.

G18. Eisenhower's Sorrow missile. From U.S. 2 at Niagara, go north 4.9 miles on State Highway 32. Missile is on the right.

G19. Thumbing a Ride missile.

From State Highway 32 at Petersburg, go east 3.6 miles on U.S. 2. Missile is on the right.

G20. Rachel Wept missile. from the intersection of County Road 1 and the road to Dahlen, go west 4 miles, then right 1 mile on County Road 5, then right .7 mile. Missile is on the right.

FLIGHT H

H0. Unfunny launch control center. From Michigan, go north 5 miles on State Highway 35. Control center is on the right.

H21. Cancer Cavities missile. From Whitman, go north .5 mile on State Highway 35, then right 1.6 miles on the section line road. Missile is on the right.

H22. TV Tower missile. From Petersburg, go north 5.5 miles on County Road 5. Missile is on the right.

H23. Winds of Hades missile. From Main Street in Petersburg, go west 2.5 miles on U.S. 2, then right .6 mile. Missile is on the right.

H24. Fizzle missile. From U.S. 2 at Michigan, go south 3.9 miles on County Road 35, then left 1.4 miles. Missile is on the right.

H25. Broken Lid missile. From Michigan, go west 2.2 miles on U.S. 2. Missile is on the left.

H26. Gopher missile. From Lakota, go east 4 miles on U.S. 2, then right .7 mile, then left .1 mile, then right 4.3 miles. Missile is on the left.

H27. Jammed Hatch missile. From U.S. 2 at Mapes Corner, go north 3.5 miles on County Road 22. Missile is on the right.

H28. Scrambled Radar missile. From U.S. 2 at Lakota, go north 3 miles on State Highway 1. Missile is on the left.

H29. Loken missile. From County Road 7 and State Highway 1 at Brocket, go south 4 miles, then left 1.6 miles. Missile is on the left.

H30. Freeze missile. From U.S. 2 at

Mapes Corner, go north 10 miles on County Road 22, then right .4 mile on County road 2. Missile is on the left.

FLIGHT I

I0. Susie-Lee-Mary 2 launch control center. From State Highways 15 and 1 at Pekin, go north 4 miles, then right .7 mile. Control center is on the left.

I31. Daddy Warbucks missile. From Petersburg, go south 4.3 miles on State Highway 32. Missile is on the left.

I32. County Line missile. From Larimore, go west 12.8 miles on County Road 4, then right 2.6 miles on County Road 9. Missile is on the right.

I33. Old Barb missile. From Petersburg, go south 7.1 miles on State Highway 32, then left 3.1 miles, then right 1.2 miles. Missile is on the left.

I34. Peaceless missile. From Larimore, go west 8.1 miles on County Road 4. Missile is on the right.

I35. McMissile missile. From just east of McVille on State Highway 15, go north 5.2 miles on County Road 35. Missile is on the right.

I36. Sheyenne River missile. From the intersection of State Highways 15 and 1, go west .3 mile on Highway 15, then left 4.4 miles on County Road 16. Missile is on the left.

I37. Eddy County missile. From the junction of State Highways 20 and 15 north of McHenry, go 1 mile north on State Highway 20, then right .6 mile. Missile is on the right.

I38. Friendly Farm missile. Just south of Tolna, from the intersection of County Road 23 and State Highway 15, go west on 15 to State Highway 20, then left 3.3 miles on Highway 20, then left 2 miles on a gravel road, then right 1 mile, then left 1.5 miles. Missile is on the right.

I39. Tons of Turkeys missile. Just south of Tolna, from the intersection

Missile silo serves as ever-present reminder at North Dakota peace school.

Margaret Mooney

of County Road 23 and State Highway 15, go west 1.1 miles on 15, then right 2 miles, then (after crossing railroad tracks) go left 1.8 miles. Missile is on the left.

I40. Stump Lake missile. From the junction of U.S. 2 and State Highway 1 at Lakota, go south 8 miles. Missile is on the right.

FLIGHT J

J0. Beatrice launch control center. From Southam, go east 4.5 miles on County Road 6. Control center is on the left.

J41. Ophelia missile. From Brocket, go west 4.1 miles on County Road 7, then right 1 mile, then right .3 mile. Missile is on the left.

J42. Titania missile. From Doyon, at intersection of U.S. 2 and Doyon Road, go east 3.6 miles on U.S. 2 to a tall tower, then left 1.8 miles, then right 1 mile, then left .2 mile. Missile is on the left.

J43. Perdita missile. From junction of U.S. 2 and County Road 4 (west of Doyon), go south 4.1 miles to a fork, then left 1.6 miles, then right .3 mile. Missile is on the left.

J44. Cleopatra missile. from junction of U.S. 2 and County Road 4

(west of Doyon), go west 2 miles on U.S. 2, then left 1.1 miles. Missile is on the left.

J45. Desdemona missile. From junction of U.S. 2 and County Road 4 (West of Doyon), go north 5.6 miles on Road 4. Missile is on the left.

J46. Cordelia missile. From U.S. 2 south of Crary, go north 3.9 miles on the Crary road, then left 1.1 miles on County Road 2. Missile is on the left.

J47. Katherina missile. From U.S. 2 south of Crary, go north 3.9 miles on the Crary road, then left 1 mile on County Road 2, then right 5.3 miles on County Road 3. Missile is on the right.

J48. Rosalind missile. From Southam, go north 3.6 miles on County Road 4. Missile is on the left.

J49. Miranda missile. From Lawton, go west 11.7 miles on County Road 8. Missile is on the right.

J50. Olivia missile. From Lawton, go west 5.9 miles on County Road 8. Missile is on the right.

FLIGHT K

K0. Charon's Ferry launch control center. From Finley, go north 6 miles on State Highway 32. Where highway turns west, go right, then left 7.3

miles. Control center is on the right.

K1. Wish it Away missile. From intersection of State Highways 18 and 15, go south 1 mile on County Road 23, then right 2 miles, then left 3.5 miles. Missile is on the left.

K2. Vishnu's Heater missile. From Finley, go north 4 miles on State Highway 32, then right 2.2 miles. Missile is on the left.

K3. Valkyrie Roulette missile. From State Highway 32 at Aneta, go east about 5 miles on the main street to a major curve to the south, then continue east 1 mile. Missile is on the right.

K4. Attila's Fantasy missile. From Aneta, go north 3.3 miles on State Highway 32, then right 3.5 miles. Missile is on the right.

K5. Prairie's Bane missile. From Aneta, go north 9 miles on State Highway 32. Missile is on the left.

K6. Golgotha missile. From the junction of State Highways 18 and 15 (northwest of Northwood), go 1 mile south on County Road 23, then right 6 miles, then left 3 miles and turn right. Missile is on the left.

K7. Caspar W.'s Ghost missile. From Petersburg, go south 9.1 miles on State Highway 32, then left 1.9 miles. Missile is on the right.

K8. Fruit of Acedia missile. From Aneta, go north 4.5 miles on State Highway 32, then right 8.1 miles on State Highway 15, then left 1 mile on County Road 16, then left .3 mile. Missile is on the right.

K9. Harry Truman's missile. From State Highway 18 just west of Kempton, go west 6 miles on County Road 6, then right .2 mile. Missile is on the right.

K10. Maginot's Folly missile. From the junction of State Highways 15 and 18 northwest of Northwood, go west 4.4 miles on Highway 15. Missile is on the right.

FLIGHT L

L0. Savage Lagoon launch control center. From Luverne, go north 5.7 miles on State Highway 32. Control center is on the right.

L11. A Fine and Private Place missile. From Finley, go south 1.3 miles on State Highway 32, then left 1.8 miles. Missile is on the right.

L12. Cancer missile. From Finley, go east 7 miles on State Highway 200. Missile is on the left.

L13. Peace Garden State missile. From Finley, go south 7.7 miles on State Highway 32, then right .2 mile on County Road 8-A. Missile is on the left.

L14. Wylie missile. From Finley, go south 4.4 miles on State Highway 32, then left 5 miles on County Road 11, then right .3 mile on County Road 6. Missile is on the left.

L15. Dumbfounded missile. From Finley, go east 10.8 miles on State Highway 200, then right 3.3 miles on County Road 8. Missile is on the right.

L16. Prairie Rose missile. From State Highway 32 and County Road 5 (road to Hope), go west 1.7 miles. Missile is on the right.

L17. Easy Come, Easy Go missile. From State Highway 32 and County Road 5 (road to Hope), go south 4.8 miles on Highway 32. Missile is on the right.

L18. Shirley missile. From north end of Luverne, go east 2.1 miles on a gravel road, then left .5 mile. Missile is on the left.

L19. C'est Fini missile. From the junction of State Highways 32 and 26 at Pillsbury, go west 5 miles on Highway 26, then left 1.1 miles. Missile is on the left.

L20. All Mine missile. From Finley, go south 4.4 miles on State Highway 32, then right 5.9 miles on State Highway 200, then left 1.8 miles. Missile is on the right.

FLIGHT M

M0. Nervous Energy launch control center. From State Highway 38 at Colgate Road, go north 2.5 miles, then

Sunset on the prairie. Weathervane is for the benefit of Air Force helicopters landing in the silo enclosure.

Wendy Weiss

left .4 mile on County Road 1. Control center is on the right.

M21. J. Denby Mercenary missile. From the junction of State Highway 38 and the railroad tracks at Buffalo, go north 4.6 miles. Missile is on the right.

M22. Prairie Road missile. From Page, go north 4.3 miles on State Highway 38, then left 2.8 miles on County Road 2, then left .7 mile on County Road 1. Missile is on the left.

M23. Homestead missile. From I-94 at Tower City, go north 6 miles, then left .1 mile. Missile is on the right.

M24. Tower View missile. From I-94 at Tower City, go north 1 mile, then left .8 mile. Missile is on the right.

M25. Burning Sage missile. From I-94 at Oriska, go north 3.2 miles. Missile is on the right.

M26. Meadowlark missile. From I-94 exit at Oriska, go north 8 miles on State Highway 32. Missile is on the left.

M27. Messier's missile. From Pillsbury, go south 8.4 miles on State Highway 32, then right .3 mile (across from electrical substation). Missile is on the right.

M28. Golden Wheat missile. From I-94 Exit 71 at Peak, go north 8.8 miles. Missile is on the right.

M29. Disarmingly Simple missile. From Pillsbury, go south 1 mile on State Highway 32. Missile is on the right.

M30. Eric's missile. From I-94 Exit 71 at Peak, go north 14.4 miles, then left 1.3 miles. Missile is on the left.

FLIGHT N

N0. Nuke Ourselves launch control center. From Dazey, go north 2.4 miles on State Highway 1. Control center is on the right.

N31. Valley View missile. From Aneta, go south 4.6 miles on State Highway 32, then right 3.8 miles. Missile is on the right.

N32. Airport missile. From State Highway 200 at Cooperstown, go south 4.7 miles on the paved airport road. Missile is on the left.

N33. Consumption missile. From State Highway 45 in Cooperstown, go east 2.7 miles on State Highway 200. Missile is on the right.

N34. Stupifaction missile. From Sharon, go west 3.2 miles on State Highway 32, then left 1 mile, then right .3 mile. Missile is on the left.

N35. Big Gold missile. From Finley, go west 6 miles on County Road 18, then left .3 mile. Missile is on the right.

N36. Life Out of Balance missile. From the post office in Hannaford, go east 4.7 miles, then right 1.5 miles. Missile is on the right.

N37. Summitry missile. From Sibley, go west 2.6 miles on State Highway 26 to a point where it starts to turn south, then go forward .8 mile, then right .8 mile. Missile is on the left.

N38. Busy Acres missile. From the junction of State Highways 200 and 1 (West) go east .3 mile on State Highway 200. Missile is on the right.

N39. Abominator missile. From State Highway 200, go south 4 miles on State Highway 1, then right 2 miles, then left 1.5 miles. Missile is on the right.

N40. Hazard missile. From the junction of State Highways 200 and 1 east, go west .8 mile on State Highway 200. Missile is on the left.

FLIGHT O

O0. Double Aught launch control center. From the junction of State Highways 200 and 45 at Cooperstown, go north 4.1 miles. Control center is on the left.

O41. Mintone missile. From the junction of State Highway 15 and Main Street at McVille, go southeast .9 mile, then left 1.8 miles. Missile is on the right.

O42. West Marshland missile. From Aneta, go north .2 mile on State Highway 32, then left 5.2 miles on County Road 20. Missile is on the left.

O43. Barizoni's Watch missile. From Aneta, go north 4.2 miles on State Highway 32, then left 2 miles on State Highway 15, then left 1 mile and left .2 mile. Missile is on the left.

O44. Gray Mourning missile. From Aneta, go south 1.3 miles on State Highway 32, then left .3 mile. Missile is on the right.

O45. Out of Mind missile. From Jessie, go west .3 mile on State Highway 65, then right 2.9 miles. Missile

is on the left.

O46. Rock Pile missile. From the junction of State Highways 65 and 1 at Binford, go north 6.3 miles, then right .8 mile. Missile is on the right.

O47. Six Bin missile. From State Highway 15 at Pekin, go south 5.2 miles on State Highway 1, then right .4 mile. Missile is on the left.

O48. Mystery missile. From State Highway 15 at Pekin, go south 4.2 miles on State Highway 1, then left 4.6 miles (keeping right) to a "T" in the road, then left .3 mile. Missile is on the right.

O49. Shelterbelt missile. From the junction of State Highways 45 and 65, go west 2 miles on Highway 65, then right 6.8 miles. Missile is on the left.

O50. Ottawa Church missile. From the junction of State Highways 45 and 65, go north 1.8 miles. Missile is on the left.

Grand Forks Silos of note

D0. About two miles south of a multi-billion-dollar Anti-Ballistic Missile site mothballed by Congress and the Pentagon soon after its completion in 1975. Dominated by a 75-foot pyramid built to house radar equipment, the facility has all the appearances of a small town: paved streets, houses, apartments, even a cathedral. It is populated by four caretakers.

E46. Site of a missile silo peace school held June 19-28, 1987. Event attracted some 250 local residents and peace activists from the United States and Canada. Workshops, held in a large meeting tent near the silo fence, dealt with the nuclear arms race, problems in agriculture, and a variety of related issues.

H24. The fizzle missile. Here, in 1968, the Air Force attempted unsuccessfully to demonstrate the launching of a Minuteman missile. Tethered to keep it from going too far, the missile was twice ignited but failed each time to leave the silo. The spectators included U.S. Senator Milton R. Young of North Dakota and a lone protester, the Rev. Robert Branconnier, chaplain at St. Thomas Newman Center, University of North Dakota, Grand Forks.

South Dakota

Minuteman-land is eerie. On the surface, no weapons are visible. But beneath the empty prairies and forested hills the gyroscopes are eternally spinning; these are the master navigators of jam-proof guidance systems, each ready to steer holocaustal destruction to a pre-selected target.

—John G. Hubbell in *The Reader's Digest*, October 1962.

Missile silo K8, near Spearfish, South Dakota

© John Hooton

Editors note: Many of the following missile silos and launch control centers are on land claimed by the Lakota Nation. In the view of many Lakota the last valid treaty between the United States and the Lakota Nation was one signed in 1868. It left all of South Dakota west of the Missouri River in Lakota hands.

FLIGHT A

A1. Pumpkin's Pride launch control center. From Quinn, go north 28.1 miles on County Road C513. Control center is on the right.

A2. Horrible Heffalump missile. From the junction of State Highways 73 and 34 at Billsburg, go west 7.2 miles on State Highway 34, then left 6.2 miles. Missile is on the left.

A3. Mordor missile. From the junction of State Highways 73 and 34 at Billsburg, go west 7.2 miles on State Highway 34, then left 6.6 miles, then left 5.1 miles, then right 1.3 miles, then left 1.7 miles. Missile is on the right.

A4. Not Even Eeyore's missile. From the junction of State Highways 73 and 34 at Billsburg, go south 8.1 miles on State Highway 73, then right 8.7 miles, then left 1.4 miles. Missile is on the right.

A5. Durin's Bane missile. From the junction of State Highways 73 and 34 at Billsburg, go west 7.2 miles on State Highway 34, then left 6.4 miles, then left 5.1 miles, then right 1.3 miles, then left 2.3 miles, then left 5.5 miles. Missile is on the left.

A6. Mourning Dove missile. From Quinn, go north 23.5 miles on County Road C513. Missile is on the right.

A7. Katzenjammer missile. From Quinn, go north 15.6 miles on County Road C513, then continue forward 2 miles on County Road T517. Missile is on the right.

A8. Sammy's missile. From Creighton, go south 1.8 miles on the Creighton Road. Missile is on the right.

A9. Nick's missile. From Creighton, go north 1 mile, then right 2.9 miles (continuing forward), then left .7 mile. Missile is on the right.

A10. Styx & Stones missile. From Creighton, go north 6.5 miles on a curvy road. Missile is on the left.

A11. Charon's Raft missile. From Creighton, go north 14.3 miles on a curvy road. Missile is on the left.

FLIGHT B

B1. Contragate launch control center. From I-90 Exit 107 (west of Wall), go north 5.5 miles. Control center is on the right.

B2. Free Parking missile. From Wall, go north 11.6 miles on Creighton Road. Missile is on the right.

B3. McNamara's missile. From Quinn, go north 10.2 miles on County Road C513. Missile is on the right.

B4. Lost in Space missile. From Wall, go north 4.1 miles on Creighton Road, then right 3.8 miles (road curves left, then right), then left .2 mile. Missile is on the left.

B5. First Strike missile. From I-90 Exit 112 (east of Wall), go east 2.2 miles on U.S. 14. Missile is on the left.

B6. Open Gate missile. From I-90 Exit 110 at Wall, go south 4.2 miles on State Highway 240. Missile is on the left.

B7. Admiral John's missile. From I-90 Exit 107 (west of Wall), go north .4 mile on Cedar Butte Road. Missile is on the right.

B8. Womb Envy missile. From I-90 Exit 110 at Wall, go south 1.5 miles on State Highway 240, then right 5 miles, then left 2 miles. Missile is on the left.

B9. General Richard's missile. from I-90 Exit 101 (east of Wasta), go south 2.2 miles on the Jensen Road. Missile is on the right.

B10. Gorbanifar's missile. From I-90 Exit 107 (west of Wall), go north then northwest 14.4 miles. Missile is on the right.

B11. Thieves and Knaves missile. From Creighton, go south 5 miles, then right 4.5 miles on County Road 501. Missile is on the right.

FLIGHT C

C1. Thermonuclear Warfare launch control center. From Philip, go north 9.3 miles on State Highway 73, then left 1.7 miles. Control center is on the right.

C2. Mike's Roadside Rest missile. From the junction of State Highways 73 and 34 at Billsburg, go south 4.9 miles on State Highway 73. Missile is on the right.

C3. The Missile Next Door missile. From Philip, go north 10.1 miles on State Highway 73, then right 3 miles, then right 2.3 miles. Missile is on the left.

C4. Darrell's Roadside Rest missile. From Philip, go north 3.4 miles on State Highway 73. Missile is on the left.

C5. Berenson's Pride missile. From Philip, go west 3.1 miles on U.S. 14. Missile is on the left.

C6. Mundt's Muff missile. From Philip, go west 7.6 miles on U.S. 14. Missile is on the right.

C7. Rural Blight missile. From Philip, go west 1 mile on U.S. 14, then right 8.3 miles immediately after crossing a bridge. Missile is on the left.

C8. Farewell to Arms missile. From Philip, go west 1 mile on U.S. 14, then right 14.3 miles immediately after crossing a bridge. Missile is on the right.

C9. The Naked missile. From Philip, go west 1 mile on U.S. 14, then right 19 miles immediately after crossing a bridge. Missile is on the right.

C10. Omnicide missile. From Philip, go north 9.1 miles on State Highway 73, then left 8.5 miles. Missile is on the left.

C11. Boeing Corporation missile. From the junction of State Highways 73 and 34 at Billsburg, go south 8.1 miles on State Highway 73, then right 3.9 miles on the road to Hilland. Missile is on the left.

FLIGHT D

D1. Mike and Beth's launch control center. From I-90 Exit 127 (west of Cactus Flats), go north .7 mile. Control center is on the left.

D2. Grindstone missile. From Cottonwood, go west 1.8 miles on U.S. 14, then right 5.1 miles on the Grindstone Road. Missile is on the right.

D3. Transfiguration Plowshares

missile. From Cottonwood, go west 1 mile on U.S. 14. Missile is on the left.

D4. Harmonic Conversion missile. From I-90 Exit 131 at Cactus Flats, go east on the southern frontage road 5.1 miles, then left 5.4 miles, passing under I-90. Missile is on the left.

D5. Lyle's Right missile. From I-90 Exit 131 at Cactus Flats, go east on the southern frontage road 5.1 miles, then left under I-90 .1 mile, then left 1.8 miles, then right .3 mile. Missile is on the right.

D6. Badlands Barry missile. From I-90 Exit 131 at Cactus Flats, go west on the southern frontage road 2 miles, then left 2 miles. Missile is on the right.

D7. Lost Vulture missile. From I-90 Exit 121 (east of Wall), go south 6.1 miles, then right 3 miles. Missile is on the left.

D8. Tom's missile. From I-90 Exit 121 (east of Wall), go south 2.2 miles. Missile is on the right.

D9. Cassandra's missile. From I-90 Exit 116 (east of Wall), go south .6 mile. Missile is on the right.

D10. Jane's missile. From Quinn, go east 3.5 miles on U.S. 14, then right 1.2 miles. Missile is on the left.

D11. Mona's missile. From Quinn, go east 3.5 miles on U.S. 14, then left 4.2 miles. Missile is on the left.

FLIGHT E

E1. The Greenhouse/Gaudete launch control center. From I-90 Exit 152 (east of Kadoka), go north 4.7 miles. Control center is on the right.

E2. Jeremy's missile. From Philip, go east 10.8 miles on U.S. 14. Missile is on the left.

E3. Sarah's missile. From I-90 Exit 163 at Belvidere, go north 5 miles. Missile is on the left.

E4. Michael's missile. From I-90 Exit 163 at Belvidere, take the southern frontage road west 3.7 miles, then right .4 mile. Missile is on the left.

E5. Carl Kline's missile. From I-90 Exit 152 (east of Kadoka), take the northern frontage road east 1 mile. Missile is on the right.

E6. Susie's missile. From I-90 Exit 150 at Kadoka, take the southern frontage road west 1.9 miles. Missile is on the left.

E7. Debbie's missile. From the junction of I-90 and State Highway 73, take the southern frontage road west 3.9 miles, then right .4 mile. Missile is on the right.

E8. Danny's missile. From I-90, go north 2 miles on State Highway 73. Missile is on the right.

E9. Mary Beth and Jim's missile. From I-90, go north 7 miles on State Highway 73. Missile is on the left.

E10. Mary's missile. From I-90, go north 6.9 miles on State Highway 73, then right 4 miles on a gravel road. At a fork, veer left 1.1 miles, then left 2.2 miles. Missile is on the right.

E11. Laurie's missile. From Philip, go east 4 miles on U.S. 14. Missile is on the right.

FLIGHT F

F1. Contra Connection launch control center. From Maurine, go west 8.1 miles on U.S. 212, then left 1.8 miles. Control center is on the left.

F2. North Forty missile. From Maurine, go west 6.4 miles on U.S. 212, then right 4.2 miles. Missile is on the left.

F3. Ollie's Folly missile. From Maurine, go west 3.7 miles on U.S. 212. Missile is on the right.

F4. Fawn's Delight missile. From Maurine, go east 1.2 miles on U.S. 212. Missile is on the left.

F5. Secord's Profit missile. From Maurine, go south 4.6 miles on County Road 31. Missile is on the left.

F6. Iran's Ire missile. From Maurine, go west 3 miles on U.S. 212, then left 5.1 miles on County Road 27. Missile is on the left.

F7. Or is It Iraq? missile. From Maurine, go south 8.7 miles on County Road 31. Missile is on the left.

F8. Remember What? missile. From Maurine, go west 3 miles on U.S. 212, then left 8 miles on County Road 27, then right 3.7 miles on County Road 28. Missile is on the right.

F9. Meese Truth missile. From Mud Butte, go south 6.1 miles on County Road 23. Missile is on the left.

F10. Reagan Knew missile. From Mud Butte, go west 3.8 miles on U.S.

212. Missile is on the right.

F11. Bush, Too missile. From Mud Butte, go east 1.5 miles on U.S. 212. Missile is on the right.

FLIGHT G

G1. The Heritage Connection launch control center. From Stoneville, go south .6 mile on County Road 27. Control center is on the left.

G2. Many Farms missile. From Redowl, go north 1.6 miles to a "Y", then right 1.1 miles, then left 3.7 miles on County Road 31B. Missile is on the left.

G3. Life's Blood missile. From Redowl, go south .7 mile on County Road 31B. Missile is on the right.

G4. Have Perished missile. From Enning, go north 3 miles on County Road 31B, then left .6 mile. Missile is on the left.

G5. Since We Began missile. From Union Center, go north 6.4 miles on County Road 27. Missile is on the right.

G6. This Destruction missile. From Fairpoint, go south 10 miles. Missile is on the right.

G7. Choices Made missile. From Fairpoint, go south 3.7 miles. Missile is on the left.

G8. Hungry Children missile. From Fairpoint, go west 6.8 miles. Missile is on the left.

G9. Will Be Gone missile. From Fairpoint, go west 2.4 miles. Missile is on the left.

G10. If Nukes Remain missile. From Fairpoint, go east 1.5 miles. Missile is on the left.

G11. Top Priority missile. From Stoneville, go north 6.3 miles on County Road 27. Missile is on the left.

FLIGHT H

H1. Hiroshima Denied launch control center. From Union Center, go west 8.4 miles on State Highway 34, then left 4.5 miles on County Road 21. Control center is on the right.

H2. Angel Dust missile. From Union Center, go west 2.9 miles on State Highway 34. Missile is on the left.

H3. George McGovern's 597 Vote missile. From Union Center, go east

Near Philip, South Dakota, all roads lead to nuclear missile silos.

1.9 miles on State Highway 34. Missile is on the right.

H4. Moscow Children's Hospital missile. From Union Center, go west .8 mile on State Highway 34, then left 4.6 miles on County Road 27. Missile is on the right.

H5. Brokedown Palace missile. From Enning, go south 4.7 miles on County Road 31. Missile is on the right.

H6. Picnic Canyon missile. From Enning, go south 9.7 miles on County Road 31. Missile is on the right.

H7. Pro-Active missile. From the Hereford fire house, go east 1.2 miles, then left .5 mile, then right 3 miles, then right 1.2 miles. Missile is on the left.

H8. Why Die? missile. From the Hereford fire house, go east 1.2 miles, then right 1 mile, then right .4 mile. Missile is on the right.

H9. Terry Peak missile. From Union Center, go west 14.4 miles on State Highway 34, then left 5.7 miles. Missile is on the left.

H10. Son of Sam missile. From Union Center, go west 13.1 miles on State Highway 34. Missile is on the left.

H11. Charles Manson's missile.

From Union Center, go west 8.4 miles on State Highway 34, then right .7 mile on County Road 23. Missile is on the left.

FLIGHT I

I1. Melting Pot launch control center. From Plainview, go west 7.4 miles on State Highway 34. Control center is on the left.

I2. Bad missile. From Marcus, go west .5 mile to County Road 26, then right 5.9 miles. Missile is on the right.

I3. Augustus Owsley Stanley III missile. From Marcus, go west .5 mile to County Road 26, then right .5 mile. Missile is on the right.

I4. Wart missile. From Plainview, go west 3.3 miles on State Highway 34. Missile is on the right.

I5. Cap the Knife missile. From Plainview, go east 1.8 miles on State Highway 34. Missile is on the right.

I6. Open Range missile. From Plainview, go south 4.5 miles on County Road 39. Missile is on the right.

I7. End of the Road missile. From Enning, go east 4.9 miles on State Highway 34, then right 4.5 miles on County Road 14B, then left 1.8 miles. Missile is on the right.

I8. Jim Abdnor's Tunnel Vision missile. From Enning, go east 3.3 miles on State Highway 34. Missile is on the right.

I9. City on a Hill missile. From White Owl, go east 1.5 miles on State Highway 34. Missile is on the left.

I10. Mustard missile. From Redowl, go north 1.7 miles, then right 5.5 miles. Missile is on the right.

I11. High Plains Panorama missile. From Marcus, go west .5 mile to County Road 26, then right 3.3 miles, then left 3.4 miles. Missile is on the left.

FLIGHT J

J1. Tear Down the Wall launch control center. From Main Street in Faith, go west 8.1 miles on U.S. 212, then left 9.7 miles on County Road 37, then right 5.6 miles. Control center is on the left.

J2. Nappin' at the Summit missile. From Main Street in Faith, go west 15.5 miles on U.S. 212. Missile is on the left.

J3. Peace Creeper missile. From Main Street in Faith, go west 10.3 miles on U.S. 212. Missile is on the right.

J4. Kissinger's Reasoning missile. From Main Street in Faith, go west 5 miles on U.S. 212. Missile is on the left.

J5. Unnamed missile. From Main Street in Faith, go west 8.1 miles on U.S. 212, then left 5.2 miles on County Road 37. Missile is on the left.

J6. Pentagonia missile. From Main Street in Faith, go west 8.1 miles on U.S. 212, then left 11.1 miles. Missile is on the right.

J7. Congressonia missile. From Main Street in Faith, go west 8.1 miles on U.S. 212, then left 15.7 miles. Missile is on the left.

J8. Thatcher's Tether missile. From Main Street in Faith, go west 8.1 miles on U.S. 212, then left 16.3 miles, then right 3.7 miles. Missile is on the left.

J9. Bush's Bet missile. From Maurine, go east 7.7 miles on U.S. 212, then right 12.4 miles on a curvy road. Missile is on the left.

J10. Caspar's Envy missile. From Maurine, go east 7.7 miles on U.S. 212, then right 5.7 miles on a curvy road. Missile is on the right.

J11. Dakota's Humiliation missile. From Maurine, go east 6.2 miles on U.S. 212. Missile is on the left.

FLIGHT K

K1. Custer's Karma launch control center. From I-90 west of Spearfish, go north 3.6 miles on U.S. 85. Control center is on the left.

K2. Lori's Intuition missile. From U.S. 85 at Belle Fourche, go east 4.1

continued on page 58

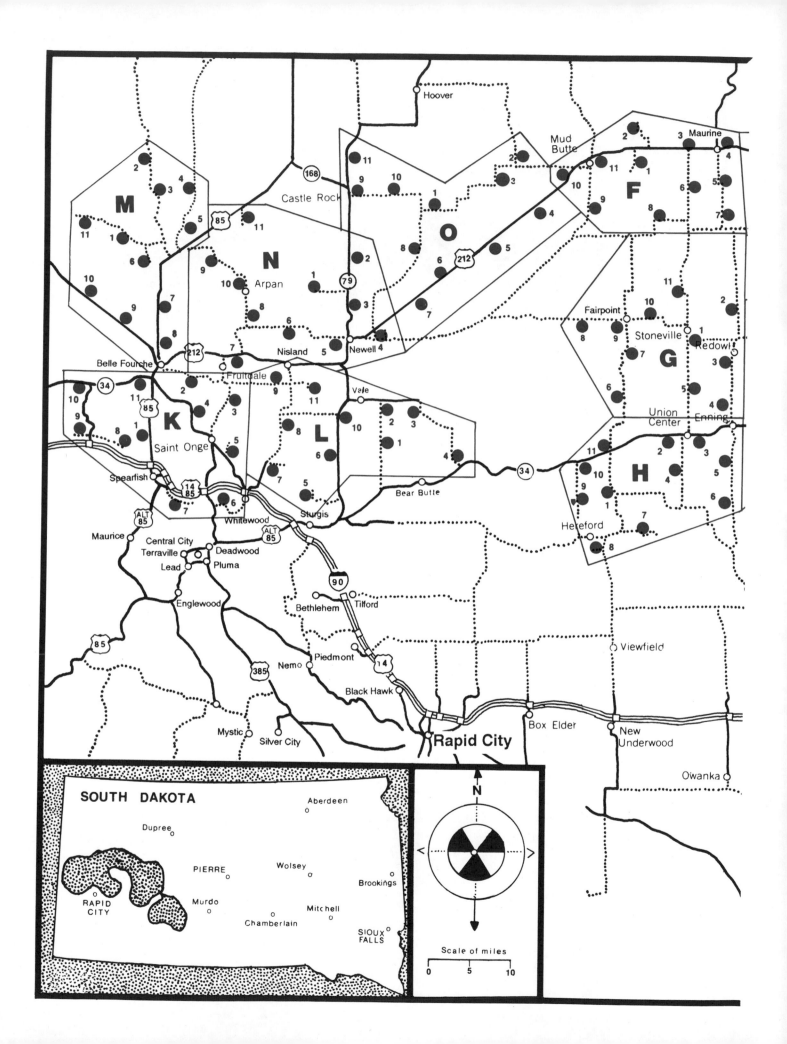

Hoover

Mud
Butte

Maurine

168

Castle Rock

M

N

O

F

Arpan

212

79

Fairpoint

Stoneville

Redowl

G

Belle Fourche

212

Nisland

Newell

Fruitdale

Vale

Union
Center

Enning

34

85

K

Saint Onge

L

Bear Butte

34

H

Spearfish

14
85

Sturgis

Whitewood

ALT
85

Hereford

ALT
85

Maurice

Central City

Terraville

Deadwood

Lead

Pluma

Englewood

90

85

Bethlehem

Tilford

385

Nemo

Piedmont

14

Viewfield

Black Hawk

Box Elder

New
Underwood

Mystic

Silver City

Rapid City

Owanka

SOUTH DAKOTA

Aberdeen

Dupree

PIERRE

Wolsey

Brookings

RAPID
CITY

Murdo

Mitchell

Chamberlain

SIOUX
FALLS

N

Scale of miles

0   5   10

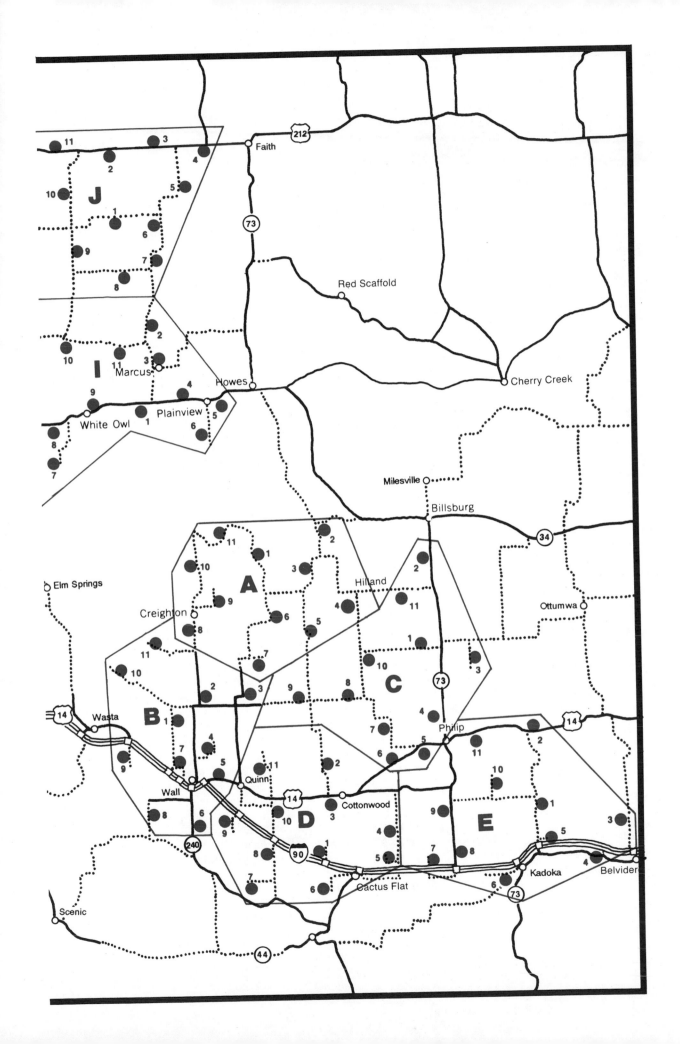

Katt/LaForge

Black Hills form the backdrop for a South Dakota Minuteman silo.

continued from page 55

miles on National Street, which turns to gravel after 2.3 miles. Missile is on the right.

K3. Bomb Bordello missile. From Saint Onge, go west .3 mile on State Highway 34, then right 2 miles to a "T", then right 3.8 miles. Missile is on the right.

K4. Tower of Babel missile. From Saint Onge, go northwest 4 miles on State Highway 34. Missile is on the right.

K5. Shellout Falter missile. From I-90 exit at Whitewood, go west 5.3 miles on State Highway 34, then right .7 mile. Missile is on the right.

K6. Posterity's Problem missile. From I-90 Exit 17, go south 2.5 miles on U.S. 85, then left 1.7 miles on a road bearing right. Missile is on the left.

K7. Politician's Prattle missile. From I-90 Exit 14, go east 2 miles on U.S. 14A. Missile is on the right.

K8. Hell Hole missile. From I-90 Exit 2, take the northern frontage road right 4 miles. Missile is on the left.

K9. The Mutt missile. From I-90 Exit 2, take the northern frontage road left 1 mile. Missile is on the right.

K10. Bane of Our Existence missile. From U.S. 85 at Belle Fourche, go west 7.4 miles on State Highway 34. Missile is on the left.

K11. Mission Impossible missile. From U.S. 85 at Belle Fourche, go west 2.7 miles on State Highway 34.

Missile is on the left.

FLIGHT L

L1. Out to Launch control center. From the post office at Vale, go east 2.9 miles, then right 5.4 miles. Control center is on the left.

L2. Prairie Tumor missile. From the post office at Vale, go east 2.9 miles, then right .3 mile. Missile is on the left.

L3. Unlit Sky missile. From the post office at Vale, go east 6.7 miles to a "T", then right 1.4 miles. Missile is on the right.

L4. Broken Arrow missile. From Bear Butte, go east 7.5 miles on State Highway 34, then left 1 mile, then right .8 mile. Missile is on the right.

L5. Lauralea-Clark missile. From the junction of State Highways 34 and 79, go north 3.2 miles on State Highway 79, then left 2.9 miles, then right .3 mile, then left 1 mile, then right .1 mile. Missile is on the left.

L6. Minds Being Wasted missile. From Vale, go west 1 mile, then left 7.4 miles on State Highway 79. Missile is on the right.

L7. Dr. Seuss missile. From I-90 exit 23, go north 4.1 miles, bearing right, then right .8 mile. Missile is on the right.

L8. Mamen's Folly missile. From I-90 exit 23, go north and bear right 9.3 miles. Missile is on the right.

L9. Regretfully Yours missile. From Nisland, go south 2 miles, then

right 2.3 miles. Missile is on the right.

L10. Orange Moon-Rise missile. From Vale, go west 1 mile, then left 2.5 miles on State Highway 79. Missile is on the left.

L11. Taxpayers' Children missile. From Nisland, go south 2 miles, then left 3 miles, then right .1 mile. Missile is on the left.

FLIGHT M

M1. No Accident launch control center. From the Belle Fourche River at Belle Fourche, go north 11.8 miles on U.S. 85, then left 2.6 miles on Camp Crook road, then left 5.7 miles on the Albion road. Control center is on the left.

M2. Meadowlark missile. From the Belle Fourche River at Belle Fourche, go north 11.8 miles on U.S. 85, then left 13.7 miles on the Camp Crook road. Missile is on the left.

M3. Brown Pelican missile. From the Belle Fourche River at Belle Fourche, go north 11.8 miles on U.S. 85, then left 8.7 miles on Camp Crook road. Missile is on the right.

M4. Velvet Buck missile. From the Belle Fourche River at Belle Fourche, go north 13.7 miles on U.S. 85, then left 8.2 miles on the Harding road. Missile is on the left.

M5. Lame Doe missile. From the Belle Fourche River at Belle Fourche, go north 13.7 miles on U.S. 85, then left 3.6 miles on the Harding road. Missile is on the right.

M6. Killdeer missile. From the Belle Fourche River at Belle Fourche, go north 11.8 miles on U.S. 85, then left 2.5 miles on the Camp Crook road, then left 2.6 miles on the Albion road, then left 2.2 miles. Missile is on the right.

M7. Kingbird missile. From the Belle Fourche River at Belle Fourche, go north 6.3 miles on U.S. 85. Missile is off the road on the right.

M8. Crow Creek missile. From the Belle Fourche River at Belle Fourche, go north 3.3 miles on U.S. 85. Missile is on the right.

M9. Twin Antelope missile. From U.S. 85 at Belle Fourche, go west 6.6 miles on U.S. 212. Missile is on the right.

M10. Prairie's Edge missile. From U.S. 85 at Belle Fourche, go west 12 miles on U.S. 212. Missile is on the right.

M11. Field of Clover missile. From the Belle Fourche River at Belle Fourche, go north 11.8 miles on U.S. 85, then left 2.6 miles on Camp Crook road, then left 11 miles on the Albion road. Missile is on the left.

FLIGHT N

N1. Human Misery launch control center. From Newell, go north 5 miles on State Highway 79, then left 4 miles. Control center is on the right.

N2. Hard Times missile. From Newell, go north 9.1 miles on State Highway 79. Missile is on the right.

N3. Small is Beautiful missile. From Newell, go north 4.6 miles on State Highway 79. Missile is on the right.

N4. More with Less missile. From Newell, go east 3.5 miles on U.S. 212, then right 1.4 miles, then left 1 mile, then left .4 mile. Missile is on the left.

N5. Fall of America missile. From the junction of State Highway 79 and U.S. 212 at Newell, go west 1.8 miles on Eighth Street. Missile is on the left.

N6. Brave New World missile. From the junction of State Highway 79 and U.S. 212 at Newell, go west 4 miles on Eighth Street, then right .7 mile, then left 2.7 miles. Missile is on the left.

N7. Crazy Bald Head missile. From Nisland, go west 7.2 miles on U.S. 212. Missile is on the left.

N8. Jah Love missile. From Nisland, go west 5.9 miles on U.S. 212, then right 5.8 miles. Missile is on the right.

N9. Livestock at Large missile. From the Belle Fourche River at Belle Fourche, go north 13.9 miles on U.S. 85, then right 3.3 miles. Missile is on the right.

N10. Amber Waves missile. From the Belle Fourche River at Belle Fourche, go north 13.9 miles on U.S. 85, then right 7.1 miles, then right 1.7 miles. Missile is on the right.

N11. Siberian missile. From the Belle Fourche River at Belle Fourche, go north 21.9 miles, then right 1.2 miles. Missile is on the left.

FLIGHT O

O1. Castle Rock launch control center. From the junction of State Highways 168 and 79, go south 1 mile on State Highway 79, then left 8 miles to a "Y", then continue left 2 miles. Control center is on the left.

O2. Supply and Demand missile. From Mud Butte, go west 1.3 miles on U.S. 212, then right 5.7 miles, then right 1.2 miles. Missile is on the right.

O3. The Gang's All Here missile. From Mud Butte, go west 1.3 miles on U.S. 212, then right 12.7 miles. Missile is on the left.

O4. Winston Smith missile. From Mud Butte, go west 9 miles on U.S. 212. Missile is on the left.

O5. Big Brother missile. From Mud Butte, go west 14.3 miles on U.S. 212. Missile is on the left.

O6. Timothy Leary missile. From Newell go east 13.6 miles on U.S. 212. Missile is on the left.

O7. Dain Bramage missile. From Newell go east 8.4 miles on U.S. 212. Missile is on the right.

O8. Be Here Now missile. From the junction of State Highways 168 and 79, go south 1 mile on State Highway 79, then left 8 miles, then right 6.6 miles. Missile is on the right.

O9. Jimi Hendrix missile. From the junction of State Highways 168 and 79, go south 1 mile on State Highway 79. Missile is on the left.

O10. Trickle Down missile. From the junction of State Highways 168 and 79, go south 1 mile on State Highway 79, then left 4.3 miles. Missile is on the left.

O11. Nuremberg . . . Ha! missile. From the junction of State Highways 168 and 79, go north 2.9 miles on State Highway 79. Missile is on the right.

South Dakota Silos of Note

E5. On April 11, 1982 (Easter Sunday), Greg Spanton, the Rev. Carl Kline, Dennis Lehmann, and the Rev. Christopher Dunphy were arrested for crossing a police line in front of this silo. Later, South Dakota Gov. William Jankow granted them a pardon to save the state the expense of trying them.

On Christmas morning, 1987, a group of Lakota Sioux from the Rosebud Reservation and non-Indian Christian supporters gathered for prayer at the silo. One of them, Charles Garriet, climbed over the fence and danced on the silo lid until Air Force guards arrived. He was charged with trespass and jailed for five days.

F8. A cave in a butte south of here is said to be the home of "Woman Who Lives with Wolves." According to a Cheyenne legend, a woman who had become separated from her tribe was rescued by a wolf, who led her to the cave and brought her food through the winter. In the spring she rejoined her people.

J6. A member of a two-man Air Force security team was shot to death by his partner on March 8, 1983, while emerging from the silo. Ellsworth Air Force Base identified the victim as Airman Daniel J. Kopp, 20, of Kansas City, Missouri. No further details were given, and the other airman was not identified.

L6. On April 2, 1988 (Easter Sunday), Kathy Jennings and Ladon Sheets, supported by a small group of Sioux and non-Indian Christians from the Rosebud Reservation, climbed the fence and placed an Easter lily on the lid of this silo, which is at the foot of Bear Butte, a sacred mountain for the Sioux nations. Convicted of trespass, they were sentenced to 15 days in jail.

L8. On April 22, 1988, Ladon Sheets was arrested for praying on the lid of this silo and sentenced to 30 days in jail on state trespass charges.

Montana

Several of the silo sites provide spectacular views of the Rocky Mountain Front; fields of ripe grain wave in the gentle wind, fences provide support for bluebird boxes. Cattle graze in grass and daisies up to their knees. Rivers wind their way through this country, small lakes dot the landscape. Haystack Butte looms in the distance, visible from four silo sites. The juxtaposition of the breathtaking pastoral beauty of the land and the silent, lurking weapons of death beneath this ground is heartbreaking.

—From *A Sightseer's Guide to Missile Silos in Lewis & Clark County*, a brochure produced by the Last Chance Peacemakers Coalition, Box 11, Helena, MT 59624.

Missile silo A4, near Monarch, Montana

© John Hooton

FLIGHT A

A1. Mountain Life Community launch control center. From the junction of U.S. 87 and State Highway 427 at Raynesford, go west 3.9 miles on U.S. 87. Control center is on the left.

A2. Joy's missile. From the center of Belt go east .2 mile on Bridge Street to the end, then left .1 mile, then right 4.1 miles, then left 3.6 miles. Missile is on the left.

A3. David's missile. From Raynesford, go east 1 mile on U.S. 87, then left 3.4 miles, then left 5.2 miles. Missile is on the right.

A4. Richard's missile. From Raynesford, go south 6.5 miles on State Highway 427. Missile is on the left.

A5. Siksikauw missile. From Monarch, go east 9.8 miles on the Dry Creek Road toward Hughesville. Missile is on the right.

A6. Tom's missile. From Monarch, go south 5.1 miles on U.S. 89. Missile is on the left.

A7. Nasen Coulee missile. From Monarch go north 5.1 miles on U.S. 89. Missile is on the left.

A8. Lucinda's missile. From Monarch, go north 11.9 miles on U.S. 89, then left 4.3 miles past Sluice Box State Monument. Missile is on the right.

A9. Perry's missile. From Stockett, go south 3.1 miles on State Highway 227, then left 3.4 miles. Missile is on the left.

A10. Nan's missile. From the junction of State Highway 331 and U.S. 89/State Highway 200 at Belt, go southwest .3 mile, then left 5.6 miles on Tiger Butte Road, then right 1.6 miles. Missile is on the right.

A11. Bryan's missile. From the center of Belt, go east .2 mile on Bridge Street to the end, then left .1 mile, then right .5 mile. Missile is on the left.

FLIGHT B

B1. The Moscow Group for Trust launch control center. From U.S. 87 at Geyser exit, go north 1 mile, then right 6 miles (road curves left), then right 1.1 miles. Control center is on the

right.

B2. Irena's missile. From Stanford, go north 12.5 miles on State Highway 80. Missile is on the right.

B3. Antipersonnel missile. From Coffee Creek, go northwest 2 miles on State Highway 81, then forward (north) 2.5 miles on a gravel road, then, when State Highway 81 turns west, go right .5 mile. Missile is on the right.

B4. Olga's missile. From the railroad tracks at Denton, go south then west .3 mile, then continue west 4.5 miles, then left .5 mile. Missile is on the right.

B5. Wolf Creek missile. From Stanford, go north 6.6 miles on State Highway 80. Missile is on the left.

B6. Surprise Creek missile. From 3rd Avenue South and U.S. 87 at Stanford, go northwest 4.8 miles on U.S. 87, then left 2.9 miles. Missile is on the left (at end of long access road).

B7. Mean-Spirited missile. From Geyser, go southeast 2.4 miles on U.S. 87. Missile is on the right.

B8. Sergei's missile. From U.S. 87 at Geyser exit, go west 3.5 miles on U.S. 87. Missile is on the left.

B9. Arrow Creek missile. From U.S. 87 at Geyser exit, go north 4.4 miles. Missile is on the right.

B10. Highwood Mountains missile. From U.S 87 at Geyser exit, go north 4.4 miles, then left 3.7 miles, then right 5 miles. Missile is on the right.

B11. Alexander's missile. From U.S. 87 at Geyser exit, go north 4.4 miles, then right 6.8 miles. Missile is on the right.

FLIGHT C

C1. Nuclear Train Campaign launch control center. From the junction of U.S. 87 and State Highway 80 at Stanford, go southeast 4.5 miles on U.S. 87. Control center is on the right.

C2. Carol's missile. From the railroad tracks and State Highway 80 at Stanford, go east then north 1.7 miles on State Highway 80, then right 4.5 miles. Missile is on the left.

C3. Sage Creek missile. From Moccasin, go north 6 miles until road turns

right, then immediately left 4 miles. Missile is on the right.

C4. Luna's missile. From Windham, go east 7 miles on U.S. 87, then left 5 miles. Missile is on the right.

C5. Mike's missile. From Utica, go east 3.3 miles on State Highway 239, then left 3.5 miles. Missile is on the left.

C6. Bipartisan missile. From Utica, go southwest, keeping right, 1 mile. Missile is on the right.

C7. Burning Bodies missile. From Utica, go southwest, keeping right, 8 miles. Missile is on the right.

C8. Montana Women Initiating Nuclear Disarmament missile. From the junction of the road to State Highway 80 and U.S. 87 west of Stanford, go south 12 miles, keeping left at all forks (pavement turns to gravel), then left 4.9 miles on Sage Creek Road. Missile is on the left.

C9. Sue's missile. From the junction of the road to State Highway 80 and U.S. 87, go south 11.6 miles, keeping left at all forks (pavement turns to gravel), then right 2.8 miles on Dry Wolf Road. Missile is on the left.

C10. Running Wolf Creek missile. From the junction of the road to State Highway 80 and U.S. 87 at Stanford, go south 6.8 miles, keeping left at all forks (pavement turns to gravel). Missile is on the left.

C11. Radiation Sickness missile. From Stanford, go northwest 1 mile on U.S. 87. Missile is on the right.

FLIGHT D

D1. Green Party launch control center. From Denton, go east 1.7 miles on State Highway 81, then left 8.6 miles on County Road 547. Control center is on the right.

D2. Bonnie's missile. From Denton, go east 1.7 miles on State Highway 81, then left 6.4 miles on County Road 547, then left 3.1 miles, then right .5 mile, then left 11.3 miles. Missile is on the right.

D3. Butch's missile. From Denton, go east 1.7 miles on State Highway 81, then left 8.8 miles on County Road 547, then right 20.5 miles. Missile is on the right.

D4. Tim's missile. From Denton, go east 1.7 miles on State Highway 81, then left 8.8 miles on County Road 547, then right 14.4 miles on County Road 547. Missile is on the left.

D5. Paul N.'s missile. From Denton go east 1.7 miles on State Highway 81, then left 8.8 miles on County Road 547, then right 6.3 miles on County Road 547. Missile is on the right.

D6. Dementia missile. From Denton, go east 16.5 miles on State Highway 81. Missile is on the left.

D7. Joe's missile. From Denton, go east 10.3 miles on State Highway 81. Missile is on the right.

D8. Jesus Wept missile. From Denton, go east 3.9 miles on State Highway 81, then right 2.8 miles. Missile is on the right.

D9. Shameless Swaggering missile. From Denton, go north 2.1 miles. Missile is on the right.

D10. Coffee Creek missile. From Denton, go north 8 miles, then left 1 mile, then right .9 mile. Missile is on the right.

D11. Blood Coulee missile. From Denton, go east 1.7 miles on State Highway 81, then left 6.4 miles on County Road 547, then left 3.1 miles, then right .5 mile, then left 4.2 miles. Missile is on the right.

FLIGHT E

E1. New Zealand Nuclear Free launch control center. From Suffolk, go south .9 mile on State Highway 236, then right .4 mile, then left 3.7 miles. Control center is on the right.

E2. Missouri River Breaks missile. From the post office at Winifred, go east 1.5 miles, passing grain elevators, then left 5.9 miles. Missile is on the left.

E3. Melting Cities missile. From Suffolk, go north 4.3 miles on State Highway 236. Missile is on the left.

Montana missile in the shadow of the Rocky Mountain Front Range.

E4. Cut Bank Creek missile. From the post office at Winifred, go east 1.5 miles, passing grain elevators, then left .5 mile, then right 2 miles, then left .9 mile, then right 2.6 miles. Missile is on the left.

E5. Rolling Hills missile. From Suffolk, go north 3.3 miles on State Highway 236, then right 5 miles, then right .9 mile. Missile is on the left.

E6. Indefensible missile. From Christina, go north 2.3 miles on State Highway 236. Missile is on the left.

E7. Moulton missile. From Hilger go north 5.5 miles on State Highway 236. Missile is on the left.

E8. North Moccasin Mountains missile. From Lewistown, go north 9 miles on U.S. 191, then left 9.5 miles on State Highway 81, then right 5 miles. Missile is on the right.

E9. Box Elder Creek missile. From Hilger, go north 6.2 miles on State Highway 236, then left 4.2 miles, then right 2 miles, then right 2.5 miles. Missile is on the right.

E10. Salt Creek Pines missile. From Suffolk, go north .6 mile on State Highway 236, then left 5.5 miles, then right 2.2 miles. Missile is on the right.

E11. Pluto's Bayonet missile. From the post office at Winifred, go north 4.6 miles on State Highway 236. Missile is on the right.

FLIGHT F

F1. Greenpeace launch control center. From the junction of County Road 434 and U.S. 287 at Augusta, go north 9.4 miles on U.S. 287. Launch control center is on the left.

F2. Burd Hill missile. From U.S. 89 at Choteau, go south 1 mile on U.S. 287, then right 2.2 miles on the Pishkon Reservoir Road. Missile is on the right.

F3. Roundup Coulee missile. From U.S. 89 at Choteau, go south 10 miles on U.S. 287. Missile is on the left.

F4. Sun River missile. From U.S. 89 at Fairfield, go west 9 miles on State Highway 408. Missile is on the right.

F5. Bickle missile. From the junction of County Road 434 and U.S. 287 at Augusta, go north 1.5 miles on U.S. 287, then right 7 miles on State Highway 21, then right .7 mile. Missile is on the right.

F6. Ramrod missile. From the junction of County Road 434 and U.S. 287 at Augusta, go north 3.3 miles on U.S. 287. Missile is on the right.

F7. Ashes In Our Mouths missile.

From the junction of County Road 434 and U.S. 287 at Augusta, go southwest 3.5 miles on County Road 434, then right .5 mile. Missile is on the left.

F8. Clemons Coulee missile. From the junction of County Road 434 and U.S. 287 at Augusta, go north 11.7 miles on U.S. 287, then left 3.7 miles, then right at a "T" 4.8 miles. Missile is on the right.

F9. Emma Goldman missile. From the junction of U.S. 89 and U.S. 287 at Choteau, go south 1 mile on U.S. 287, then right 5.4 miles on Pishkon Reservoir Road, then left 11.5 miles, Missile is on the left.

F10. Arms Control missile. From the junction of U.S. 89 and U.S. 287 at Choteau, go south 1 mile on U.S. 287, then right 13.8 miles on Pishkon Reservoir Road. Missile is on the right.

F11. Willow Creek missile. From the junction of U.S. 89 and U.S. 287 at Choteau, go south 1 mile on U.S. 287, then right 5.4 miles on Pishkon Reservoir Road, then left 5.5 miles. Missile is on the right.

FLIGHT G

G1. Last Chance Peacemakers Coalition launch control center. From the junction of State Highway 200 and U.S. 287, go north 4.3 miles on State Highway 200. Control center is on the left.

G2. Iron Hill missile. From the junction of State Highways 200 and 21, go south 8.4 miles on State Highway 200. Missile is on the right.

G3. St. John's Creek missile. From I-15 Exit 256 at Cascade, go northwest 6.9 miles on St. Peter Mission Road, then right 6.3 miles. Missile is on the left.

G4. White Wind Stone missile. From I-15 Exit 256 at Cascade, go northwest 6.9 miles on St. Peter Mission Road. Missile is on the left.

G5. St. Peter Mission missile. From I-15 Exit 256 at Cascade, go northwest 6.9 miles on St. Peter Mission Road, then left at "Y" 6 miles. Missile is on the left.

G6. Twin Bridge Coulee missile. From the junction of U.S. 287 and State Highway 200, go south 6 miles on U.S. 287, then left 2 miles. Missile is on the left.

G7. Auchard Creek missile. From the junction of U.S. 287 and State Highway 200, go south 5.5 miles on State Highway 200. Missile is on the left.

G8. Wrangle Creek missile. From the junction of U.S. 287 and State Highway 200, go south 8.5 miles on State Highway 200, then right 5.5 miles on County Road 434. Missile is on the left.

G9. Flat Creek missile. From the junction of U.S. 287 and State Highway 200, go north 4.5 miles on U.S. 287. Missile is on the right.

G10. Dry Creek missile. From the junction of County Road 434 and U.S. 287 at Augusta, go south 5.3 miles on \U.S. 287, then left 2.5 miles. Missile is on the right.

G11. Simms Creek missile. From the junction of State Highway 200 and U.S. 287, go north 7.7 miles on State Highway 200, then left 6.5 miles, then left 1 mile. Missile is at dead end.

FLIGHT H

H1. Greenham Common Women's Peace Camp launch control center. From the junction of U.S. 89 and State Highway 408 at Fairfield, go north 3.5 miles on U.S. 89, then right 1.8 miles, then right 2 miles on "5th Road North," then left .8 mile. Control center is on the right.

H2. Living Hell missile. From the junction of I-15 and State Highway 221 at Dutton, go west 3.7 miles on State Highway 221, then left 3.4 miles. Missile is on the right.

H3. Fairfield Bench missile. From I-15 Exit 302 at Power, go west 3.2 miles on State Highway 431, then continue west 2.8 miles on gravel. Missile is on the left.

H4. We Don't Think About It missile. From the junction of State Highway 200 and U.S. 89 east of Sun River, go northwest .2 mile on U.S. 89, then right (at the church) 5 miles, then right 1 mile, then left .5 mile, then right .6 mile. Missile is on the left.

H5. Hillside missile. From the junction of State Highway 200 and U.S. 89 east of Sun River, go northwest 7.1 miles on U.S. 89, then left .3 mile. Missile is on the right.

H6. Shaw Butte missile. From the post office at Fort Shaw, go south .4 mile on pavement to an intersection, then continue south 2.8 miles on gravel. Missile is on the right.

H7. Humankind Booby-Trapped missile. From the junction of State Highways 200 and 21 at Simms, go south 1.8 miles on State Highway 200. Missile is on the right.

H8. Butte Canal missile. From the junction of State Highways 200 and 21 at Simms, go west 7 miles on State Highway 21. Missile is on the right.

H9. Starving Millions missile. From the junction of U.S. 89 and State Highway 408 at Fairfield, go west 2.6 miles on State Highway 408. Missile is on the right.

H10. Priest Butte missile. From the junction of U.S. 89 and U.S. 287 at Choteau, go south 2.2 miles on U.S. 89, then right 3.5 miles. Missile is on the right.

H11. Big Sky missile. From the junction of State Highway 221 and U.S. 89 at Choteau, go east 8.8 miles on State Highway 221, then continue forward .2 mile, then right 2.3 miles. Missile is on the right.

FLIGHT I

I1. Save All Living Things launch control center. From I-15 Exit 256 at Cascade, go south .8 mile on State Highway 68, then left 12.5 miles on Central Ave. (State Highway 330), then left 6.6 miles. Control center is on the right.

I2. Extreme Prejudice missile. From Eden, go southwest 1 mile. Missile is on the left.

I3. Spanish Coulee missile. From I-15 Exit 256 at Cascade, go south .8 mile on State Highway 68, then left 12.5 miles on Central Avenue (State Highway 330), then right 2.3 miles. Missile is on the right.

I4. Bird Creek missile. From I-15 Exit 256 at Cascade, go south .8 mile on State Highway 68, then left 6.3 miles on Central Avenue (State Highway 330), then right 8.2 miles on Adel Road. Missile is on the left.

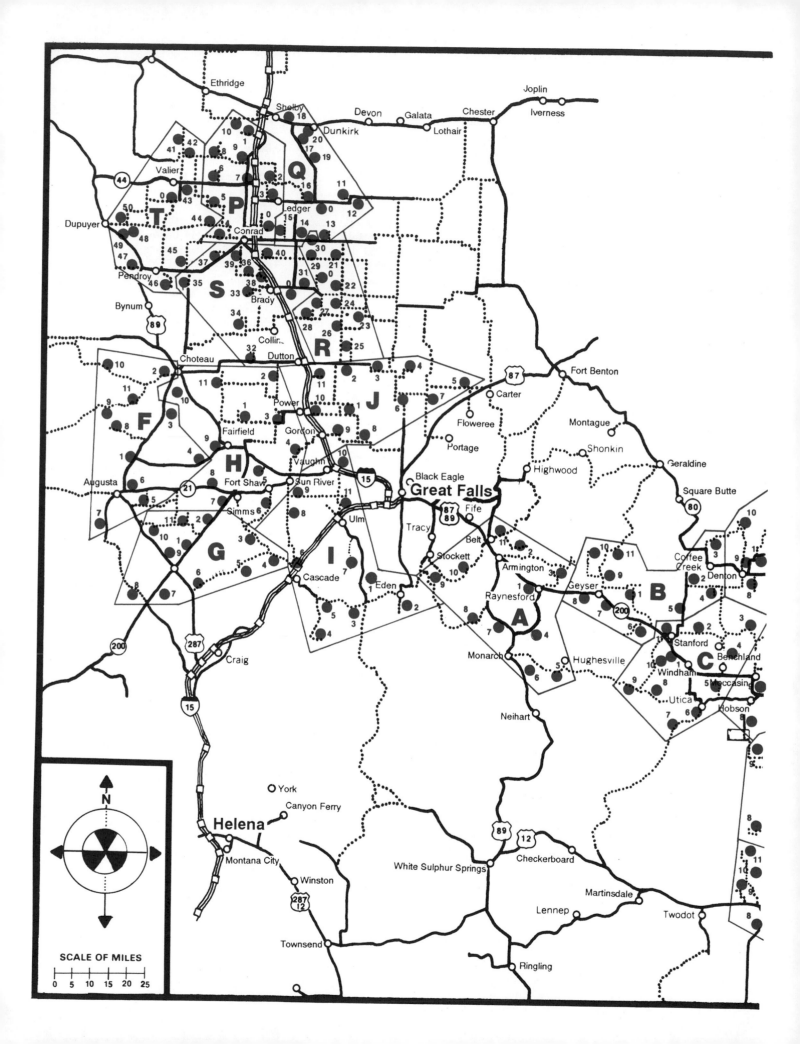

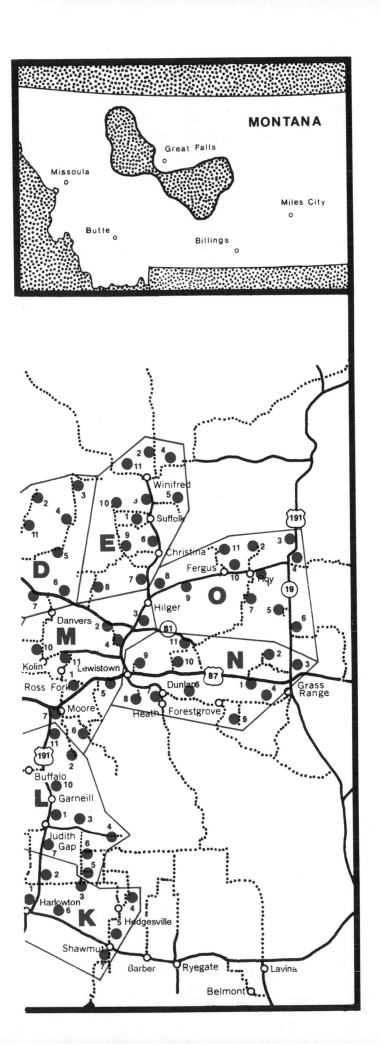

I5. Cameron missile. From I-15 Exit 256 at Cascade, go south .8 mile on State Highway 68, then left 7.5 miles on Central Avenue (State Highway 330). Missile is on the right.

I6. Hate Filled missile. From I-15 Exit 256 at Cascade, go northeast .8 mile on northern frontage road, then left .6 mile. Missile is on the right.

I7. Muddy Creek missile. From I-15 Exit 270 at Ulm, go south 4 miles on State Highway 330, then right .4 mile, then left 2 miles. Missile is at dead end.

I8. Square Butte missile. From Sun River, go south 8.7 miles on pavement just west of the river. Missile is on the left.

I9. Blind Worship missile. From Sun River go south 2.8 miles on pavement just west of the river. Missile is on the left.

I10. American Dream missile. On the east side of the junction of I-15 Exit 290 and U.S. 89/State Highway 200.

I11. Money Is No Object missile. From I-15 Exit 270 at Ulm, go north 2.2 miles, then left .5 mile, then right 1 mile, then right .5 mile. Missile is on the right.

FLIGHT J

J1. Easter Peace Celebration launch control center. From I-15 Exit 302 at Power, go north 2 miles on western frontage road, then right (under I-15) 4 miles, then left 1 mile, then right 1.6 miles. Control center is on the right.

J2. John's missile. From I-15 Exit 313 at Dutton, go south .6 mile on east frontage road, then left 8 miles on State Highway 379. Missile is on the right.

J3. Spencer Coulee missile. From I-15 Exit 313 at Dutton, go south .6 mile on the east frontage road, then left 13.2 miles on State Highway 379, then right at a "T" 1.5 miles (turning left). Missile is on the left.

J4. Cheryl's missile. From I-15 Exit 313 at Dutton, go south .6 mile on the east frontage road, then left 13.2 miles on State Highway 379, then right 1 mile, then left 3.8 miles, then right 1 mile, then left 2 miles, then left 1 mile, then right 1.2 miles. Missile is on the left.

J5. Decent, God-Fearing missile. From the U.S. 87 bridge over the Missouri River at Black Eagle, go northeast 21.4 miles on U.S. 87, then left (opposite Floweree Road) 1.9 miles, then left 2 miles. Missile is on the right.

J6. Bootlegger Trail missile. From the U.S. 87 bridge over the Missouri River at Black Eagle, go northeast 9.4 miles, then left (north) 8.1 miles, then left 5.7 miles. Missile is on the left.

J7. Huntley Coulee missile. From the U.S. 87 bridge over the Missouri River at Black Eagle, go northeast 9.4 miles, then left (north) 7.8 miles. Missile is on the right.

J8. Benton Lake missile. From I-15 Exit 297 at Gordon, go east 8 miles, then left 3 miles. Missile is on the right.

J9. Terry's missile. From I-15 Exit 297 at Gordon, go east 2.9 miles. Missile is on the left.

J10. Power Crazy missile. From I-15 Exit 302 at Power, go east .1 mile, then left .1 mile. Missile is on the left.

J11. Darla's missile. From I-15 Exit 313 at Dutton, go south 3.2 miles on the eastern frontage road, then left 1 mile. Missile is on the left.

FLIGHT K

K1. General Assembly to Stop the Powerline to Minnesota launch control center. From the junction of U.S. 12 and U.S. 191 North at Harlowton, go north 1 mile on U.S. 191. Control center is on the left.

K2. Innumerable Kiloton missile. From the junction of U.S. 12 and U.S. 191 North at Harlowton, go north 7 miles on U.S. 191. Missile is on the right.

K3. Roberts Creek missile. From the junction of U.S. 12 and U.S. 191 North at Harlowton, go north 6.5 miles on U.S. 191, then right 7.1 miles, then right 1.7 miles. Missile is on the right.

K4. Honored and Glorified missile. From Shawmut, go north 8.7 miles on State Highway 297, then right .8 mile at a "T", crossing Careless Creek, then left 1 mile. Missile is

on the right.

K5. Hilltop missile. From Shawmut, go north 3.5 miles on State Highway 297. Missile is on the right.

K6. Mussellshell River missile. From the junction of U.S. 12 and U.S. 191 North at Harlowton, go east 6 miles on U.S. 12. Missile is on the left.

K7. Mud Creek missile. From Shawmut, go south 2.8 miles. Missile is on the right.

K8. Crazy Mountain View missile. From the junction of U.S. 12 and U.S. 191 South at Harlowton, go south 4.7 miles on U.S. 191. Missile is on the right.

K9. Mexican John Creek missile. From the junction of U.S. 12 and U.S. 191 South at Harlowton, go west 5.2 miles on U.S. 12, then right 1 mile, then left 3 miles, then left 1.4 miles. Missile is on the right.

K10. Spring Prairie Flower missile. From the junction of U.S. 12 and U.S. 191 South at Harlowton, go west 1.1 miles on U.S. 12, then right 6.7 miles. Missile is on the right.

K11. Hopley Creek Gulch missile. From the junction of U.S. 12 and U.S. 191 South at Harlowton, go west 1.1 miles on U.S. 12, then right 15 miles. Missile is on the right.

FLIGHT L

L1. Charter 77 of Czechoslovakia launch control center. From the junction of U.S. 191 and the railroad tracks at Judith Gap, go north 1.6 miles on U.S. 191. Control center is on the right.

L2. Little Trout Creek missile. From U.S. 87 at Moore, go south 4 miles, then left 1 mile, then right 2.3 miles, then left 3.1 miles, keeping left at forks. Missile is on the right.

L3. Escalation Dominance missile. From the junction of U.S. 191 and State Highway 297 at Judith Gap, go east 6.5 miles on State Highway 297. Missile is on the left.

L4. Timber Creek missile. From the junction of U.S. 191 and State Highway 297 at Judith Gap, go east 13 miles on State Highway 297. Missile is on the right.

L5. Little Careless Creek missile. From the junction of U.S. 12 and U.S.

191 at Harlowton, go north 6.5 miles on U.S. 191, then right 11 miles, then left 3 miles, then right 1 mile. Missile is on the right.

L6. Blake Creek missile. From the junction of U.S 191 and State Highway 297 at Judith Gap, go east 6.8 miles on State Highway 297, then right 5.9 miles, then continue forward 1.4 miles. Missile is on the left.

L7. Armed Robbery missile. from the junction of U.S. 191 and the railroad tracks at Judith Gap, go south 4.6 miles on U.S. 191. Missile is on the left.

L8. Stevens Gulch missile. From the junction of U.S. 191 and the railroad tracks at Judith Gap, go .3 mile south on U.S. 191, then right 3.2 miles, then right 3 miles, then right 1.1 miles. Missile is on the right.

L9. Buffalo missile. From Hobson, go west .8 mile on State Highway 239, then left 12.4 miles on State Highway 400. Missile is on the left.

L10. Mass Executioner missile. From the junction of U.S. 191 and the railroad tracks at Judith Gap, go north 8.5 miles on U.S. 191. Missile is on the right.

L11. Heartless missile. From the junction of U.S. 87 and U.S. 191 west of Moore, go south 6.3 miles on U.S. 191. Missile is on the left.

FLIGHT M

M1. Latin American Christian Base Communities launch control center. From Moore, go northeast 4 miles on U.S. 87/191. Control center is on the left.

M2. Brian's missile. from the junction of U.S. 191 and State Highway 81 north of Lewistown, go west 6.5 miles on State Highway 81. Missile is on the left.

M3. Warm Spring Creek missile. From the junction of U.S. 191 and State Highway 81 north of Lewistown, go north 1 mile on U.S. 191. Missile is on the right.

M4. Molten Bones missile. From the junction of U.S. 191 and 87 at Lewistown, go north 4.5 miles on U.S. 191, then left 1 mile. Missile is on the right.

M5. Nuclear Gulag missile. From

the center of Lewistown, go west 5 miles on U.S. 87/191. Missile is on the left.

M6. Amy's missile. From U.S. 87 at Moore, go south 1 mile, then left 4 miles, then right 1.2 miles, then left 1 mile, then right .7 mile, then left 1.1 miles. Missile is on the right.

M7. Massacre at Moore missile. From the junction of U.S. 87 and U.S. 191 west of Moore, go south .2 mile on U.S. 191. Missile is on the left.

M8. Cumulative and Irreversible missile. From Hobson, go west .8 mile on State Highway 239, then left 5.4 miles on State Highway 400. Missile is on the left.

M9. Chernobyl Cubed missile. From Moccasin, go southeast 2.4 miles on U.S. 87. Missile is on the left.

M10. Moral Asphyxia missile. From the west end of Kolin, go north 2.2 miles. Missile is on the left.

M11. Hanover missile. From the junction of U.S. 191 North and U.S. 87 at Lewistown, go north 2.4 miles on U.S. 191, then left 10.3 miles on State Highway 426, then left .8 mile, then right 1.6 miles. Missile is on the right.

FLIGHT N

N1. Nukewatch launch control center. From the junction of U.S. 87 and State Highway 19 north of Grassrange, go west 11 miles on U.S. 87. Control center is on the left.

N2. Chippewa Creek missile. From the junction of U.S. 87 and State Highway 19 north of Grassrange, go north 2 miles on State Highway 19, then left 6.4 miles, then right 1.2 miles. Missile is on the right.

N3. Cauterized Conscience missile. From the junction of U.S. 87 and State Highway 19 north of Grassrange, go north 2.8 miles on State Highway 19. Missile is on the right.

N4. Becket missile. From Grassrange, go south on Main, crossing a bridge, then right .4 mile to a fork, then right 7 miles. Missile is on the right.

N5. Bear Creek missile. From Grassrange, go south on Main, crossing a bridge, then right .4 mile to a fork, then right 12 miles, then left 4.7 miles. Missile is on the right.

N6. Ungodly Cynical missile. From the railroad tracks south of Lewistown, go southeast 8.5 miles on State Highway 238, then left 7.6 miles. Missile is on the left.

N7. Atrocities on Command missile. From the railroad tracks at the south end of Lewistown, go south 7.3 miles on State Highway 238, then right 1.1 miles, then left .6 mile, keeping left at forks. Missile is on the right.

N8. Iron Heel missile. From the railroad tracks at the south end of Lewistown, go south .8 mile on State Highway 238, then right .4 mile on a residential street, then left 4.1 miles on pavement that turns to gravel. Missile is on the left.

N9. Unsanitary Landfill missile. From Meadowlark Lane east of Lewistown, go east 1.7 miles on U.S. 87, then left .3 mile. Missile is on the right.

N10. Mark's missile. From Meadowlark Lane east of Lewistown, go east 12.9 miles on U.S. 87, then left 1.7 miles. Missile is on the right.

N11. Maiden Creek missile. From Meadowlark Lane east of Lewistown, go east 12.9 miles on U.S. 87, then left 5.8 miles, then right 4.9 miles. Missile is on the left.

FLIGHT O

O1. Polish Freedom and Peace Groups launch control center. From Roy, go east 1.3 miles on U.S. 191. Control center is on the right.

O2. Stomping Nightmare missile. From Roy, go north 7 miles. Missile is on the left.

O3. Sacogawea missile. From Roy, go east 7.4 miles on U.S. 191, then left 6.4 miles on U.S. 191. Missile is on the left.

O4. Terrorism's Icon missile. From Roy, go east 7.4 miles on U.S. 191, then right .5 mile on State Highway 19, then left .8 mile. Missile is on the left.

O5. Burton K. Wheeler missile. From the junction of U.S. 87 and State Highway 19 north of Grassrange, go north 15.6 miles on State Highway 19, then left 1.1 miles, then left .9 mile. Missile is on the right.

O6. Little Box Elder Creek missile. From the junction of U.S. 87 and State Highway 19 north of Grassrange, go north 8.5 miles on State Highway 19. Missile is on the right.

O7. Moral Novocaine missile. From Roy, go south 8 miles, keeping right. Missile is on the left.

O8. Unforgivable missile. From Hilger, go east 3.4 miles on U.S. 191. Missile is on the left.

O9. Minuteman's Slaughterhouse missile. From Hilger, go east 9.7 miles on U.S. 191. Missile is on the right.

O10. Guilded Gas Oven missile. From Roy, go west 4.3 miles on U.S. 191. Missile is on the right.

O11. Armells Creek missile. From Fergus, go north 3.7 miles, then right 4.5 miles. Missile is on the right.

FLIGHT P

P0. Silo Pruning Hooks launch control center. From Conrad, go east 1 mile on State Highway 218, then left

The Rev. Ed Bigler (center) at Ed's Missile west of Peetz, Colorado.

2.1 miles on the frontage road, then right .4 mile. Control center is on the left.

P1. Bear River missile. From I-15 Exit 358 (Marias River Road) south of Shelby, go west .8 mile. Missile is on the right.

P2. Martin's missile. From I-15 Exit 345 (Ledger Road), go east 2.4 miles on State Highway 366, then left 4.1 miles, then right 2 miles, then left 1.7 miles. Missile is on the left.

P3. Poison Dart missile. From I-15 Exit 345 (Ledger Road), go east 2.4 miles on State Highway 366, then left 1.2 miles. Missile is on the right.

P4. Sam George Hill missile. From Conrad, go west 2.8 miles on State Highway 534, then continue west 3 miles. Missile is on the right.

P5. William's missile. From the junction of Business 15 and State Highway 534 at Conrad, go west 4.5 miles on State Highway 534, then continue north 3.6 miles past railroad tracks, then left 2.9 miles, then continue forward 2.7 miles to a "T", then right .4 mile. Missile is on the right.

P6. Paul's missile. From I-15 Exit 348 (Valier Road), go west 8.3 miles on State Highway 44, then right 2

miles, then left .3 mile. Missile is on the left.

P7. Helen's missile. From I-15 Exit 348 (Valier Road), go west 1.8 miles on State Highway 44. Missile is on the right.

P8. Larry's missile. From I-15 Exit 352 (Bullhead Road) north of Conrad, go west 6 miles on the Bullhead Road, keeping left at 3.7 miles, then right at school house 1.7 miles. Missile is on the left.

P9. Carl's missile. From I-15 Exit 352 (Bullhead Road) north of Conrad, go west .5 mile, then right .6 mile on old U.S. 91. Missile is on the left.

P10. Northern missile. From I-15 Exit 358 (Marias River Road) south of Shelby, go east .1 mile, then left 3.5 miles on the frontage road, then left under I-15, then left .3 mile, then right 4.8 miles. Missile is on the left.

FLIGHT Q

Q0. Philippine People Power launch control center. From the railroad tracks at Ledger, go east 9.4 miles on State Highway 366. Control center is on the right.

Q11. Nigel's missile. From the railroad tracks at Ledger, go east 15.4

miles on State Highway 366, then left 1.1 miles, then left .8 mile. Missile is on the right.

Q12. Kate's missile. From the railroad tracks at Ledger, go east 19.1 miles on State Highway 366. Missile is on the right.

Q13. Rifle Shot missile. From Conrad , go east 19.2 miles on State Highway 218, then left 3 miles, then left .3 mile. Missile is on the left.

Q14. John's missile. From Conrad, go east 11.5 miles on State Highway 218, then left 2.2 miles. Missile is on the right.

Q15. Jim's missile. From Conrad, go east 7.2 miles on State Highway 218, then left 3.4 miles. Missile is on the left.

Q16. Thornton's missile. From the railroad tracks at Ledger, go east 4.1 miles on State Highway 366, then left .8 mile. Missile is on the right.

Q17. Greg's missile. From the railroad tracks at Shelby, go east 5 miles on U.S. 2, then right 3.7 miles on State Highway 417, then left .3 mile. Missile is on the right.

Q18. Murder-Suicide missile. From the railroad tracks at Shelby, go east 3.4 miles on U.S. 2. Missile is on

Close-up view of the lid of a Minuteman missile silo, with farm in background.

'This Sacred, Holy Ground'

A prayer read at silo I4 by Carol Collins of Great Falls on May 24, 1986, during a missile silo tour by eight Montana peace activists:

Today we stand together before this instrument of death and we envision in its place a field of growing grain. We pray for forgiveness for our complicity in violence, whether it be expressed in our thoughts, our words or our actions. We ask for guidance and strength from the Great Spirit some of us call God, knowing that this same Spirit blessed both us and the earth as we stand here today, helping heal our wounds.

We pray that all members of humanity will choose to live in harmony with one another despite our differences. We choose today to cherish our individual uniqueness as we contemplate this sacred, holy ground.

May all land where nuclear warheads sit poised for deadly missions revert back to its natural state, and may we who stand here reaffirm our faith in the basic goodness of humanity and in our creative capacity to find nonviolent solutions to conflicts we face. May our life-affirming symbols we place here today replace the symbol of death enclosed within this fence.

Allow our vision today to encompass a world of compassion, justice and reverence for all life, and may our prayers of peace help make possible the return of this hallowed ground as a source of nourishment and beauty.

Blessed be this land.

the left.

Q19. Will's missile. From the railroad tracks at Shelby, go east 5 miles on U.S. 2, then right 9.3 miles on State Highway 417. Missile is on the left.

Q20. Dunkirk missile. From the railroad tracks at Shelby, go east 8.1 miles on U.S. 2. Missile is on the right.

FLIGHT R

R0. Silence One Silo launch control center. From I-15 Exit 328 at Brady, go east 11.5 miles on State Highway 365, then left 4.6 miles. Control center is on the right.

R21. Linda's missile. From I-15 Exit 335 north of Brady, go east 19.2 miles. Missile is on the left.

R22. Karl's missile. From I-15 Exit 328 at Brady, go east 16.4 miles on State Highway 365, then left 2.3 miles. Missile is on the left.

R23. The Knees Butte missile. From I-15 Exit 328 at Brady, go east 16.4 miles on State Highway 365, then right 4 miles, then left 4.8 miles. Missile is on the right.

R24. Dung missile. From I-15 Exit 328 at Brady, go east 16.4 miles on State Highway 365, then right 2.5 miles. Missile is on the right.

R25. Llama Ranch missile. From I-15 Exit 313 at Dutton, go south .6 mile on the east frontage road, then left 10.2 miles on State Highway 379, then left 4.1 miles. Missile is on the left.

R26. Teton River missile. From I-15 Exit 321 at Collins, go east 10 miles, then right 2.3 miles. Missile is on the right.

R27. LaVonne's missile. From I-15 Exit 328 at Brady, go east 11.5 miles on State Highway 365, then right 1.7 miles. Missile is on the right.

R28. Taproot of Violence missile. From I-15 Exit 321 at Collins, go east 3.9 miles, then left .7 mile. Missile is on the left.

R29. David Hastings missile. From I-15 Exit 335 north of Brady, go east 11.5 miles. Missile is on the left.

R30. Mark's missile. From Conrad, go east 16.1 miles on State Highway 218. Missile is on the left.

FLIGHT S

S0. Plowshares Disarmament Community launch control center. From I-15 Exit 328 at Brady, go east 1.7 miles on State Highway 365. Control center is on the right.

S31. Rocky Coulee missile. From I-15 Exit 328 at Brady, go east 7 miles on State Highway 365. Missile is on the left.

S32. Teton Ridge missile. From I-15 Exit 313 at Dutton, go west 11.4 miles on State Highway 221, then left 1 mile, then left .8 mile. Missile is on the left.

S33. Muddy Creek missile. From I-15 Exit 328 at Brady, go west .8 mile to the water tower, then left .2 mile, then right 1 mile, then left 2.5 miles. Missile is on the right.

S34. Plutocrat's missile. From I-15 Exit 321 at Collins, go west 3.7 miles, then left 1.8 miles to Collins, then right 4.9 miles, then right 1 mile, then left 2.4 miles. Missile is on the left.

S35. Farmers Coulee missile. From U.S. 89 at Pendroy, go east 8.3 miles on State Highway 219, then right 2.2 miles on State Highway 220. Missile is on the right.

S36. King of Prussia 8 missile. From I-15 Exit 328 at Brady, go west .5 mile, then right .7 mile parallel to the railroad tracks, then left 7 miles. Missile is on the right.

S37. Pondera Oil Field missile. From the junction of Business 15 and State Highway 219 at Conrad, go west 5.8 miles on State Highway 219, then right 1.6 miles. Missile is on the left.

S38. State Religion missile. From I-15 Exit 328 at Brady, go west .5 mile, then right 3.4 miles parallel to the railroad tracks, then left .5 mile, then right .1 mile. Missile is on the left.

S39. Harmful If Swallowed missile. From the junction of Business 15 and State Highway 219 at Conrad, go southwest .3 mile on State Highway 219, then left 1.3 miles. Missile is on the right.

S40. Windbreaks missile. From I-15 Exit 335 at Midway, go east 2.4 miles, then left .8 mile. Missile is on the right.

FLIGHT T

T0. Big Mountain Resistance launch control center. From Valier, go east 2 miles on State Highway 44, then right 5.3 miles, curving around Lake Frances, then right 2.2 miles. Control center is on the right.

T41. Compassion's Mortuary

missile. From Valier, go north 3 miles on State Highway 358, then continue north 2.2 miles, then right 1.9 miles, then left 4.7 miles. Missile is on the left.

T42. Columbia River Fish-In missile. From Valier, go north 3 miles on State Highway 358, then continue north 2.2 miles, then right 1.9 miles, then right .1 mile. Missile is on the left.

T43. Boeing's Finest missile. From the railroad tracks at Valier, go east 1.7 miles on State Highway 44. Missile is on the right.

T44. Flathead Nation Nuclear Free Zone missile. From the junction of Business 15 and State Highway 534 at Conrad, go west 12.7 miles on curvy State Highway 534. Missile is on the right.

T45. Fat Buffalo missile. From

U.S. 89 at Pendroy, go east 7.3 miles on State Highway 219, then left 3.2 miles. Missile is on the left.

T46. Naked Militarism missile. From U.S. 89 at Pendroy, go east 1.9 miles on State Highway 219, then right 1.3 miles, then left 1 mile, then right .6 mile. Missile is on the right.

T47. Grizzly Bear missile. From the junction of U.S. 89 and State Highway 219 west of Pendroy, go west 1.3 miles on State Highway 219, then right 1.3 miles. Missile is on the right.

T48. Table Rocks missile. From the junction of U.S. 89 and State Highway 534 at Dupuyer, go east 8.5 miles on State Highway 534. Missile is on the right.

T49. Dry Fork of Marias River missile. From the junction of U.S. 89 and State Highway 534 at Dupuyer, go southeast 4.9 miles on U.S. 89.

Missile is on the left.

T50. Coyote missile. From the junction of U.S. 89 and State Highway 534 at Dupuyer, go east 4.8 miles on State Highway 534, then left 2.1 miles, then left .6 mile. Missile is on the left.

Montana
Silos of Note

A1. Launch control center for the first U.S. Minuteman nuclear missile silos, activated in the fall of 1962. Used by President Kennedy as his "ace in the hole" during the Cuban missile crisis of October, 1962.

A5. Situated on U.S. Forest Service land in the scenic Little Belt Mountains, and said to be occupied by an Indian spirit seen by Air Force maintenance workers.

E2. A 75-ton Air Force truck rolled over on its side on a county road while transporting a Minuteman missile to Malmstrom Air Force Base at Great Falls on August 28, 1985. The driver, Staff Sgt. George Pearson, 26, was injured and underwent surgery on his left elbow. It took several days for a repair crew to cut into the overturned trailer, take the missile apart and transport it in separate pieces to the air base.

E5. Along the route taken by the Nez Perce band led by Chief Joseph fleeing the U.S. cavalry out of Idaho in 1877. Other missile silos along this route are N2, N4, O7, O10 and O11.

F6. Along the route taken by Capt.

Meriwether Lewis in 1806 on the return leg of the Lewis and Clark Expedition dispatched by President Jefferson to explore the Louisiana Territory. Other missile silos along this route are F10, F11, G8, I6, I7, P2, P8, Q0, Q16, T41, T47 and T49.

G5. Along the Mullan Road, an historic highway from Fort Benton, Montana, through the Bitterroot Mountains to Walla Walla, Washington, completed in 1860 to open up the Pacific Northwest to white settlement. Other missile silos along this route are G6, I8 and I9.

G8. Along the Old North Trail, an ancient foot path running north and south along the Rocky Mountain Front, believed to have been in use for more than 12,000 years.

H7. Site of first missile silo civil disobedience in Montana. Becky Owl and Lucinda Buren-Host were arrested on August 6, 1979, for trespassing on rancher's land on their way to the silo.

I6. One silo where the Air Force and the Boeing Corporation conducted experiments in 1968-72 to test the ability of missile launch sites to withstand the electromagnetic pulse (EMP) from nuclear detonations. The tests are sus-

pected to have contributed to the cancer deaths of several workers and ranchers. A lawsuit filed by survivors was thrown out after the Air Force withheld technical information.

Q12. Four miles west of an unfinished radar site for an Anti-Ballistic Missile system, abandoned in 1972.

P1. Site of the "Little Peace Camp on the Prairie," July 1983 and July 1985, on land owned by Zane and Gloria Zell. In the summer of 1984 a tree was planted next to the silo as a first step toward an eventual peace park. The silo is the site of frequent peace gatherings by the Zell family and others.

R29. Since January 1982, a focus of the Silence One Silo campaign. More than a dozen arrests since June 5, 1982, when Mark Anderlik and Karl Zanzig were apprehended and jailed for eating bread and sowing wheat atop the silo lid. Site of many other activities, including peace camps in 1983, 1984 and 1985.

Missouri

The Weppners have three children; so do the McNiffs. Both mothers say the hardest part of living with a missile in the back forty has been explaining it to the kids. "There comes a time, usually when they are still quite young," says Mary Weppner, "when they want to know what it's all about." Recently, Wann McNiff, 10, asked the difficult questions. "She came to me and said, 'Mommy, I don't want to die,'" says Beth McNiff. "When you hear that, it breaks your heart. You wonder: Why should a child have to think about nuclear war? On the other hand, growing up in Ground Zero is not like growing up someplace else...." "We tell them," says Mary, "that at least we won't be around for the aftermath."

—Todd Brewster in *Life* magazine, November 1986.

Missile silo O3, near Knob Noster, Missouri.   © John Hooton

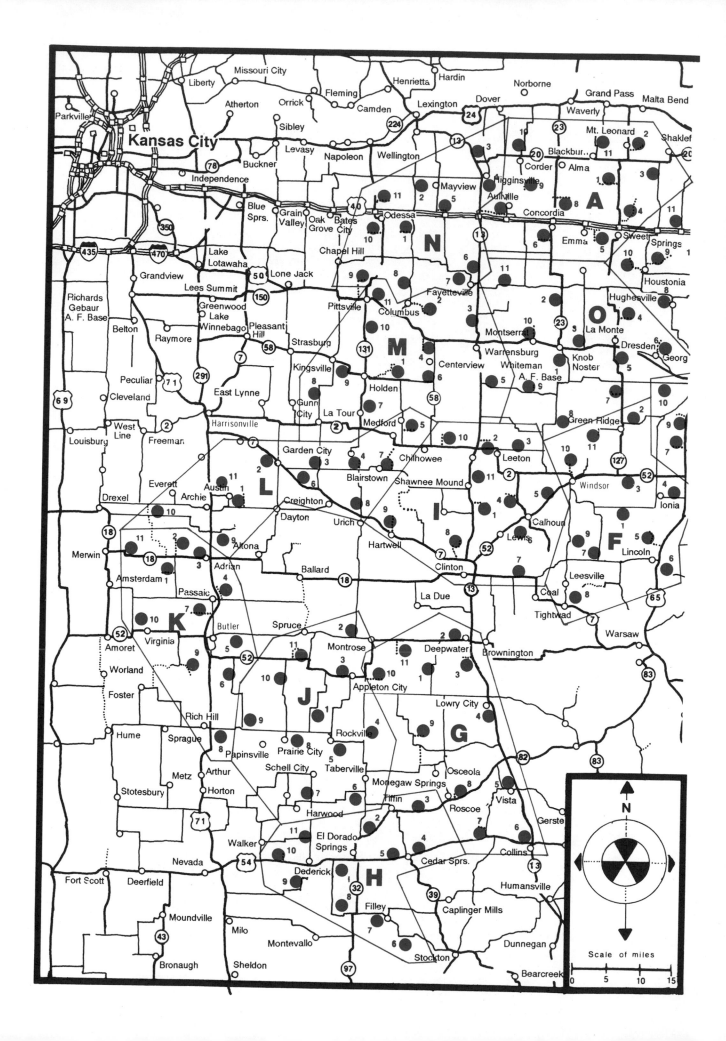

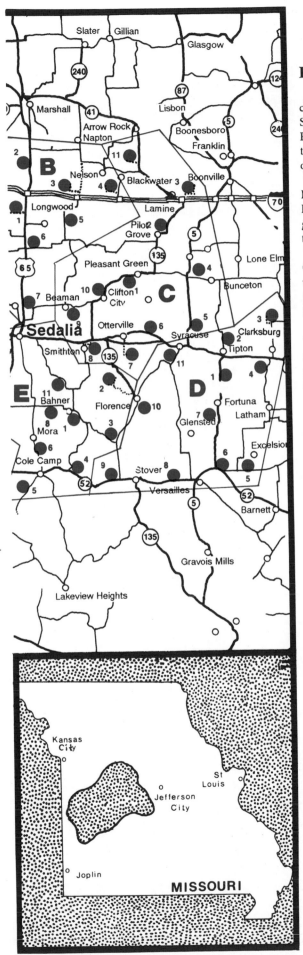

FLIGHT A

A1. Smothered Conscience launch control center. From I-70 at Sweet Springs, go north 6.2 miles on State Highway 127, then left 1.3 miles through Elmwood. Control center is on the right.

A2. The Death of Us missile. From Mt. Leonard, go south .6 mile on State Highway 127, then left 1.2 miles on a gravel road, keeping left. Missile is on the left.

A3. Blind Pony missile. From County Road Z at Shackleford, go west 2 miles on State Highway 20, then left 2.2 miles on County road EE. Missile is on the right.

A4. Take It Away missile. From I-70 at Sweet Springs, go north .7 mile on State Highway 127, then right 2.6 miles on County Road ZZ. Missile is on the left.

A5. Burns and Lacerations missile. From the junction of I-70 and County Road Y at Emma, go east 1.7 miles on the southern frontage road, then go right .4 mile. Missile is on the left.

A6. Gillam's missile. From I-70 at Concordia, go south 2.1 miles on State Highway 23 to County Road PP, then right .7 mile on a gravel road. Missile is on the right.

A7. My missile. From the junction of I-70 and County Road T south of Aullville, take the northern frontage road west .6 mile. Missile is on the right.

A8. Lose It missile. From I-70 north of Concordia, go north 3.5 miles on State Highway 23, then right .5 mile on County Road NN. Missile is on the right.

A9. Oddity missile. From Corder, go south 3.4 miles on County Road V, continuing south past the junction of County Road AA. Missile is on the left.

A10. Jane's missile. From Corder, go north 2.4 miles on County road V, which becomes County Road BB. Missile is on the left.

A11. Black missile. From State Highway 20 at Blackburn, go north .9 mile on Main Street (curving east, then north) to a junction, then go left

.9 mile. Missile is on the right.

FLIGHT B

B1. Military launch control center. From I-70, go south 2.3 miles on U.S. 65, then right 1.5 miles on County Road CC. Control center is on the right.

B2. Save the People missile. From I-70, go north 5 miles on U.S. 65. Missile is on the left.

B3. Stay Down missile. From I-70 at Napton exit, go north .2 mile on County Road J, then left 2 miles, then right .5 mile. Missile is on the left.

B4. Before You Go missile. From I-70 at Blackwater exit, go north .2 mile on County Road K to County Road Z, then left 2.3 miles, then right .2 mile. Missile is on the right.

B5. Minard's missile. From I-70 at the Napton exit, go south 5.5 miles on County Road J. Missile is on the left.

B6. Another missile. From the junction of U.S. 65 and U.S. 50 at Sedalia, go north 11.2 miles to County Road J, then go right .4 mile on J. Missile is on the left.

B7. Not Well missile. From junction of U.S. 65 and U.S. 50 at Sedalia, go north 5.3 miles on U.S. 65. Missile is on the right.

B8. Huge missile. From Hughesville, go north .7 mile on County Road H, then left 2 miles on County Road D. Missile is on the left.

B9. We're History missile. From County Road OO at Houstonia, go north .9 mile on County Road K, then right 2.7 miles on County Road CC. Missile is on the left.

B10. Over the Cliff missile. From County Road K at Houstonia, go north and west 2.8 miles on County Road OO. When paved road curves west, continue forward .8 mile. Missile is on the left.

B11. All Done missile. From I-70 at Exit 74 (8 miles east of Sweet Springs), go north 1.1 miles on County road YY. Missile is on the left.

FLIGHT C

C1. Unpleasant launch center. From County Road BB at Clifton City, go east 6.5 miles on State Highway 135. Control Center is on the

Farm machinery near the access road to silo D4, near Tipton, Missouri.

right.

C2. Anti-property missile. From County Road M in Pilot Grove, go north 1.4 miles on State Highway 135. Missile is on the left.

C3. Lela's missile. From I-70 Exit 98, go north on State Highway 135 over the overpass, then right .3 mile, then left .4 mile, keeping left. Missile is on the left.

C4. Thomas Eagleton missile. From Bunceton, go west 3 miles on County Road J, then right 1.3 miles on State Highway 5. Missile is on the right.

C5. Pounce On missile. From Syracuse, go east .9 mile on U.S. 50, then left 4.3 miles on State Highway 5. Missile is on the right.

C6. Toy missile. From County Road BB at Otterville, go northeast 4.5 miles on County Road A, then right .4 mile. Missile is on the left.

C7. More of the Same missile. From Otterville, go south 1 mile past the railroad tracks on Cherry Street. Cross U.S. 50, then continue .5 mile, then left .3 mile. Missile is on the left.

C8. Smith's missile. From the railroad tracks at the east end of Smithton, go north .2 mile on County Road W, then right, then immediately left, and go .3 mile. Missile is on the right.

C9. Pass the Buck missile. From County Road O at Beaman, go east .4 mile on County Road HH. Missile is on the right.

C10. Animal Rights missile. From County Road BB at Clifton City, go east .7 mile on State Highway 135. Missile is on the left.

C11. Located missile. From Blackwater, go northeast 2.6 miles on County Road K, then left 1.2 miles on State Highway 41, then left .3 mile on a gravel road. Missile is on the right.

FLIGHT D

D1. Tip Over launch control center. From U.S. 50 at Tipton, go south 2.9 miles on State Highway 5. Control center is on the left.

D2. Tonnage missile. From Tipton, go north 1.7 miles on County Road B. Missile is on the right.

D3. Colton missile. From Clarksburg, go north 2.6 miles on County Road H. Turn left, then immediately right 1.1 miles on a gravel road. Missile is on the right.

D4. Earl's missile. From County Road H south of Clarksburg, go west .5 mile on U.S. 50, then left .2 mile on County Road E. Missile is on the right.

D5. Excel missile. From Versailles, go north on State Highway 5 to State Highway 52, then east .7 mile on State Highway 52, then left 4.2 miles on County Road C. Missile is on the left.

D6. Versed missile. From State Highway 52 at the east end of Versailles, go north .9 mile on State Highway 5. Missile is on the right.

D7. Fortune missile. From Fortuna, go south 2.4 miles on State Highway 5, then turn right .1 mile. Missile is on the right.

D8. Versatile missile. From State Highway 5 west of Versailles, go west 3.4 miles on State Highway 52. Missile is on the right.

D9. Shove It missile. From County Road N at Stover, go west 2.7 miles on State Highway 52. Missile is on the right.

D10. Hidden missile. From County Road BB at the south end of Florence, go south 1 mile on State Highway 135. Missile is on the left.

D11. Cause It missile. From U.S. 50 at Syracuse, go south 1 mile on County Road D. Missile is on the right.

FLIGHT E

E1. Ban It launch control center. From Bahner, go east on County Road V to County Road M, then right .8 mile. Control center is on the right.

E2. Flat Creek missile. From Florence, go north on State Highway 135, then left 5.8 miles on County Road DD, then right. Missile is on the left.

E3. Pay It Out missile. From County Road JJ at Florence, go 6.6 miles south on State Highway 135, then right .5 mile on County Road M. Missile is on the right.

E4. Crock of missile. From the center of Cole Camp, go east 3.5 miles on State Highway 52, then left 1 mile on County Road A. Missile is on the right.

E5. Cold missile. From State Highway 52 at Cole Camp, go south 2.1 miles on County Road F. Missile is on the right.

E6. More missile. From State Highway 52 at Cole Camp, go north 2.7 miles on County road U, then right on County Road JJ, then immediately left .9 mile on a gravel road. Missile is on the right.

E7. Manila missile. From U.S. 50 in Sedalia, go south 9.6 miles on U.S. 65, then right 1.9 miles on a gravel road. Missile is on the right.

E8. Spring Fork missile. From Bahner, go west 4.1 miles on County Road V. Missile is on the left.

E9. Sedate It missile. From U.S. 50 at Sedalia, go south 5.5 miles on U.S.

65, then right .3 mile on County Road F. Missile is on the left.

E10. Dated missile. From U.S. 50 at Sedalia, go south .5 mile on U.S. 65, then right 4.9 miles on County Road Y. Missile is on the left.

E11. Eat It missile. From County Road V at Bahner, go north 5.5 miles on County Road M. Missile is on the left.

FLIGHT F

F1. Abandon It launch control center. From the three-way stop at Ionia, go west 7.3 miles on County Road P. Control center is on the left.

F2. Slime missile. From Green Ridge, go north .8 mile on State Highway 127, then right 2 miles on County Road B. Missile is on the left.

F3. Ill missile. From State Highway 2 at Windsor, go east 7.4 miles on State Highway 52. Missile is on the right.

F4. Exit missile. From Ionia, go east 1.9 miles on County Road P. Missile is on the left.

F5. Abe's missile. From County Road C at Lincoln, go north 2.7 miles on U.S. 65, then left 1.5 miles on County Road HH. Then turn right 1.4 miles and left .6 mile. Missile is on the left.

F6. Presidential Directive missile. From County Road C at Lincoln, go south .9 mile on U.S. 65. Missile is on the left.

F7. Pale Pinto missile. From Leesville, go north 2.8 miles on County Road PP, then right 4.7 miles on County Road C, then left 1.3 miles on County Road E. Missile is on the left.

F8. Tightwad missile. From State Highway 7 at Tightwad, go north 1.6 miles on County Road PP. Missile is on the right.

F9. D. Brook Bartlett missile. From Leesville, go north 2.8 miles on County Road PP, then continue forward 3.7 miles on County Road Y. Missile is on the right.

F10. Winds of War missile. From State Highway 52 at Windsor, go north .3 mile on State Highway 2, then right 1.4 miles on County Road WW, then left .2 mile. Missile is on the

right.

F11. Fudge missile. From State Highway 127 at Green Ridge, go west 3.3 miles on County Road B, then left .4 mile on a gravel road. Missile is on the right.

FLIGHT G

G1. Sue's launch control center. From State Highway 13 near Deepwater, go west 3.6 miles on State Highway 52, then left 5.6 miles on County Road F. Control center is on the right.

G2. Deepwater missile. From State Highway 13 near Deepwater, go west 2.9 miles on State Highway 52. Missile is on the right.

G3. Hot Water missile. From State Highway 52 near Deepwater, go south 3.2 miles on State Highway 13, then right .3 mile. Missile is on the left.

G4. Low Down missile. From County Roads A and C north of Lowry City, go south 2.5 miles on State Highway 13. Missile is on the right.

G5. Awful missile. From Vista, go west 1 mile on County Road V, then right .3 mile on County Road WW. Missile is on the right.

G6. Call for Help missile. From State Highway 13 at Collins, go west 1 mile on U.S. 54. Missile is on the right.

G7. Clark and Mary Beth's missile. From Collins, go west 6.7 miles on U.S. 54, then right 1.3 miles on County Road V, then left .2 mile. Missile is on the left.

G8. Raygun missile. From County Road E at Roscoe, go east 1 mile on State Highway 82, then left .1 mile on a gravel road. Missile is on the right.

G9. Take It missile. From County Road YY 2 miles north of Monegaw Springs, go west 2 miles on County Road B, then right 5.8 miles on County Road M, then right 1 mile on a gravel road. Missile is on the left.

G10. Zip missile. From County Roads P and KK at Appleton City, go east 1.8 miles on State Highway 52, then right .3 mile on County Road A, then left 2.2 miles on County Road AA. Missile is on the left.

G11. William Casey's missile.

From Montrose, go east 3.8 miles on State Highway 52, then right .8 mile on a gravel road. Missile is on the left.

FLIGHT H

H1. No More Cheese launch control center. From State Highway 82 south of El Dorado Springs, go west 2.5 miles on U.S. 54, then left .3 mile on County Road HH. Control center is on the left.

H2. Ruins missile. From County Road EE at El Dorado Springs, go north 2 miles on State Highway 82, then left 1.2 miles on County Road H. Missile is on the right.

H3. Rot missile. From County Road O at Tifflin, go east 3.8 miles on State Highway 82. Missile is on the left.

H4. See Saw missile. From Cedar Springs, go east 1.2 miles on U.S. 54. Missile is on the left.

H5. Choncho missile. From Cedar Springs, go west 3 miles on U.S. 54. Missile is on the right.

H6. Marc's missile. From County Road K at Filley, go east 3 miles on State Highway 32. Missile is on the right.

H7. Fill It missile. From County Road K at Filley, go west 2.3 miles on State Highway 32. Missile is on the left.

H8. Molly's missile. From County road K at Dederick, go east 3.6 miles on U.S. 54, then right 5.9 miles on County Road HH. Missile is on the left.

H9. Mary's missile. From U.S. 54 at Dederick, go south 3.8 miles on County Road K. Missile is on the right.

H10. Dead Like missile. From County Road K at Dederick, go west 3.5 miles on U.S. 54, then right .5 mile. Missile is on the left.

H11. Children's missile. From U.S. 54 at Dederick, go north 4.3 miles on County Road AA. Missile is on the left.

FLIGHT I

I1. Close It Down launch control center. From County Road CC at Shawnee Mound, go south 3 miles on State Highway 13, then left .2 mile. Control center is on the right.

I2. Shanghai missile. From County Road CC at Shawnee Mound, go north 7.2 miles on State Highway 13, then right 1 mile on a gravel road. Missile is on the right.

I3. Tons of missile. From State Highway 2 at Leeton, go east 3.2 miles on County Road EE. Missile is on the left.

I4. Big Mo missile. From State Highway 52 at Calhoun, go northwest 4.7 miles on County Road J, then left .4 mile. Missile is on the left.

I5. No Pal of Mine missile. From State Highway 2 at Windsor, go west 4 miles on State Highway 52. Missile is on the right.

I6. Nuclear Free missile. From County Road J at Calhoun, go west 2.5 miles on State Highway 52. Missile is on the left.

I7. Crumby missile. From State Highways 13 and 18 east of Clinton, go east 6.3 miles on State Highway 7. Missile is on the left.

I8. Ladon, Kathy & Erny's missile. From State Highway 13 at Clinton, go north 5.6 miles on State Highway 7, then right 1.6 miles on County Road O, then right 1.5 miles. Missile is on the left.

I9. Drudge missile. From State Highway 7 at Hartwell, go north 1.8 miles on County Road DD. Missile is on the left.

I10. Depression missile. From County Road F at Chilhowee, go east 2.7 miles on State Highway 2, then left 1.3 miles. Missile is on the right.

I11. Oppression missile. From County Road CC at Shawnee Mound, go north 1.9 miles on State Highway 13. Missile is on the right.

FLIGHT J

J1. Roy's launch control center. From Rockville, go west 4 miles on County Road B, then right 3.7 miles on County Road W. Control center is on the right.

J2. Wasted missile. From State Highway 52 at Montrose, go west 2.1 miles on County Road K, then right .5 mile on County Road K. Missile is on the left.

J3. Nobody's missile. From County Roads P and KK at Appleton City, go

Heavily guarded payload transporter leaves a missile silo enclosure.

Katt/LaForge

northwest 1.3 miles on State Highway 52. Missile is on the right.

J4. Eve of Destruction missile. From Rockville, go east 3.9 miles on County Road B, then left 2.3 miles on County Road H. Missile is on the right.

J5. Times Are Changing missile. From Rockville, go east .3 mile on County Road B. Missile is on the right.

J6. Universal Soldier missile. From Taberville, go south 1.5 miles on County Road H, then right 2 miles on County Road Y. Missile is on the left.

J7. We Want Our Rights missile. From County Road RA at Schell City, go south 2.1 miles on County Road AA. Missile is on the right, just north of County Road Y.

J8. Sweet Sympathy missile. From Prairie City, go north 1 mile on County Road O, then right .1 mile on County Road B. Missile is on the right.

J9. The Road to Find Out missile. From U.S. 71 at Rich Hill, go east 5 miles on County Road B, then left 2.25 miles on County Road N. Missile is on the right.

J10. Underground Railroad missile. From County Roads P and KK at Appleton City, go west 8.8 miles on State Highway 52, then left 3.3 miles on County Road O. Missile is on the right.

J11. Resistance missile. From Appleton City, go west 7.7 miles on

State Highway 52, then right 1.1 miles, then right .3 mile. Missile is on the right.

FLIGHT K

K1. George's launch control center. From Adrian, go west 4 miles on State Highway 18, then left 2.9 miles on County Road FF, then right 1.7 miles. Control center is on the right.

K2. Drain missile. From Adrian, go west 4 miles on State Highway 18, then right 3.6 miles on County Road FF. Missile is on the right.

K3. Dump It missile. From Adrian, go west 2 miles on State Highway 18. Missile is on the right.

K4. Pass It Up missile. From Business U.S. 71 at Passaic, go east .3 mile on County Road F, then left 1.6 miles on the frontage road. Missile is on the right.

K5. No Business missile. From Business U.S. 71 at Butler, go east 4 miles on County Road H. Missile is on the right.

K6. Colleen's missile. From U.S. 71 south of Butler, go east 4.2 miles on State Highway 52, then right 2.3 miles on County Road N. Missile is on the right.

K7. Ache missile. From County Road F at Passaic, go southeast 2 miles on Business U.S. 71, then right 3.5 miles on County Road TT. Missile is on the right.

K8. For the Rich missile. From U.S. 71 at Rich Hill, go east .6 mile on

County Road B. Missile is on the right.

K9. Jerry and Joe's missile. From U.S. 71 at Butler, go west 3.4 miles on State Highway 52, then left 3.4 miles on County Road K, then left 1.3 miles. Missile is on the left.

K10. Virgin missile. From County Road C at Virginia, go west 2 miles on State Highway 52, then right 2.3 miles on County Road J. Missile is on the right.

K11. Go Far Away missile. From Merwin, go east 3.5 miles on State Highway 18. Missile is on the left.

FLIGHT L

L1. All Sin launch control center. From Austin, go south 1 mile on County Road T, then left 2.2 miles on County Road B, then left 1.1 miles. Control Center is on the left.

L2. Harried missile. From County Roads Z and F at Garden City, go north 1.5 miles on State Highway 7. Missile is on the left.

L3. No Tours missile. From County Roads Z and F and State Highway 7 at Garden City, go east 5.6 miles on County Road N, then left 2.2 miles on County Road ZZ. Missile is on the left.

L4. Henry's missile. From Blairstown, go west 2.8 miles on County Road N, then right 2.3 miles on County Road B. Missile is on the left.

L5. The lies missile. From County Road F at Chilhowee, go west 3.5 miles on State Highway 2, then right 2.5 miles on County Road O, then right .6 mile. Missile is on the left.

L6. No Garden missile. From the junction of County Roads Z, N and F north of Garden City, go east 4.5 miles on State Highway 7. Missile is on the left.

L7. Air missile. From Blairstown, go south then east 1.7 miles on County Road N, then left .6 mile on County Road O. Missile is on the left.

L8. Itch missile. From State Highway 7 at Urich, go north 2.8 miles on County Road B. Missile is on the left.

L9. No Thank You missile. From State Highway 18 east of Adrian, go north 3.4 miles on U.S. 71, then right 1.5 miles. Missile is on the right.

L10. Too Bad We Found It missile. From Everett, go south 1 mile on County Road W, then right 3.8 miles on County Road A. Missile is on the left.

L11. Your Sons missile. From Archie, go north 2.7 miles on U.S. 71. Missile is on the right.

FLIGHT M

M1. John's launch control center. From State Highway 58 at Holden, go east 2.7 miles on County Road U. Control center is on the right.

M2. Colon missile. From Columbus, go east 3.3 miles on County Road UU, then left .8 mile. Missile is on the left.

M3. For the Birds missile. From U.S. 50 at Warrensburg, go north 4.8 miles on State Highway 13. Missile is on the left.

M4. Brian's missile. From State Highway 58 west of Warrensburg, go west .8 mile on U.S. 50, then left 1.1 miles. Missile is on the left.

M5. Steve and Judy's missile. From U.S. 50 at Warrensburg, go south 4.9 miles on State Highway 13, then left .9 mile on County Road Y. Missile is on the left.

M6. Norm and Nancy's missile. From Centerview, go south 3.2 miles on State Highway 58. Missile is on the right.

M7. Sick Bed missile. From Medford, go north 1.1 miles on State Highway 131. Missile is on the right.

M8. Gun missile. From Kingsville, go south 3.1 miles on County Road T, then right 1.8 miles on County Road TT, then left .8 mile. Missile is on the right.

M9. The King's missile. From State Highway 131 at Holden, go west 4 miles on State Highway 58. Missile is on the left.

M10. The Pits missile. From U.S. 50 at Pittsville, go south 4.3 miles on State Highway 131. Missile is on the left.

M11. Vile missile. From State Highway 131 at Pittsville, go east 1.75 miles on U.S. 50. Missile is on the left side of the divided highway.

FLIGHT N

N1. Helen and Carl's launch control center. From I-70 Exit 41, go south 2.5 miles on County Road M, then right .1 mile. Control center is on the right.

N2. Dottie's missile. From I-70 Exit 41, go north 4.7 miles on County Road O. Missile is on the right.

N3. Ken's missile. From County Road AA at Higginsville, go north 1 mile on State Highway 20/13, then right on State Highway 20, then immediately left 2 miles on State Highway 213. Missile is on the left.

N4. Hitch missile. From the junction of County Road AA and State Highway 20 at Higginsville, go south 2.4 miles on Business State Highway 13. Missile is on the left.

N5. Pruning Hooks missile. From I-70 Exit 45, go north .1 mile on County Road H, then left .2 mile on the frontage road. Missile is on the right.

N6. James Richard Sauder missile. From I-70, go south 4.2 miles on State Highway 13. Missile is on the right.

N7. Ear-ache missile. From Fayetteville, go north 3.3 miles on County Road H, then left .3 mile. Missile is on the left.

N8. Blinded missile. From County Road UU at Columbus, go north 3 miles on County Road M. Missile is on the left.

N9. Peter and Paul's missile. From State Highway 131 at Pittsville, go west 1.8 miles on U.S. 50, then right 3.1 miles, then right .5 mile. Missile is on the left.

N10. No Life missile. From 2nd and Mason Streets in Odessa, go south 2.4 miles on State Highway 131, then right 1.8 miles. Missile is on the right.

N11. Martin's missile. From I-70 near Odessa, go north 1.7 miles on State Highway 131, then right .2 mile. Missile is on the left.

FLIGHT O

O1. White Man's launch control center. Located on Whiteman Air Force Base.

O2. Lana's missile. From U.S. 50 at

Knob Noster, go north 8 miles on State Highway 23. Missile is on the left.

O3. Holly's missile. From State Highway 23 and County Road J at Knob Noster, go east 3 miles on U.S. 50, then left 2.2 miles on County Road FF, then left .1 mile. Missile is on the left.

O4. The Family missile. From the railroad tracks in La Monte, go north 3.9 miles on State Highway 127, then right .9 mile. Missile is on the left.

O5. Don't Do It missile. From U.S. 50 at La Monte, go south .7 mile on State Highway 127. Missile is on the left.

O6. Twisted, Sightless Wrecks of Men missile. From U.S. 50 in

Dresden, go north and east 1.6 miles on County Road T. Missile is on the right.

O7. Scott's missile. From U.S. 50 at La Monte, go south 6.8 miles on State Highway 127, then right .9 mile on County Road AA, then right .4 mile. Missile is on the left.

O8. Soldier Blues missile. From Knob Noster, go east 1 mile on U.S. 50, then right 10.5 miles on County Road D. Missile is on the left.

O9. Mindless missile. From State Highway 23 at Knob Noster, go east 1 mile on U.S. 50, then right 7.4 miles on County Road D, then right 4.2 miles on County Road Y, then right .3 mile. Missile is on the left.

O10. Ranger's missile. From U.S.

50 at Montserrat, go north 1.9 miles on County Road P. Missile is on the left.

O11. Jeff's missile. From U.S. 50 at Warrensburg, go north 6.7 miles on State Highway 131, then right 4.2 miles on County Road E. Missile is on the left.

Missouri
Silos of Note

B7. The children's missile. Designated as a base camp for families during an overnight missile silo vigil sponsored by Missouri peace groups on November 9, 1985. Participants spent the night at about 30 missile silos in west central Missouri.

I8. On May 1, 1986, Ladon Sheets, Kathy Jennings, and Erny Davies were arrested for praying on the silo lid. Held in jail until May 23, they re-entered the silo on May 27 and were again arrested. A federal judge sentenced them to five months, 29 days in jail.

K9. On August 5, 1987, Joe Gump and Jerry Ebner cut their way into the fenced enclosure, poured blood in the shape of a cross, and used hammers and bolt cutters to damage the silo lid and electrical outlets. Following trial and conviction on charges of property damage, Gump was sentenced to 30 months and Ebner to 40 months in prison. (Gump and his wife Jean, sentenced to eight years for damaging another Missouri missile silo in 1986 (see M6), are the parents of 12 children, all grown.)

M3. On April 13, 1982, James Richard Sauder was arrested for climbing the fence and conducting a religious service with a cross. He was sentenced to six months in prison for violating probation imposed after a similar trespass at a Titan missile site near Conway, Arkansas.

M6. On March 28, 1986 (Good Friday), two "Silo Plowshares" activists—Ken Rippetoe and John Volpe—broke into the enclosure, spray-painted, poured blood, and caused damage with sledgehammers. Three other members of the group—Darla Bradley, Larry Morlan, and Jean Gump—simultaneously undertook a similar "disarmament action" at missile silo M10. Following trial and conviction on several charges, Judge Elmo B. Hunter imposed sentences of eight years each on Darla Bradley, Larry Morlan, Jean Gump and Ken Rippetoe, and seven years on John Volpe. In 1987 Bradley, Rippetoe and Volpe were released on probation.

M10. Site of the "Silo Plowshares" action on March 28, 1986. (See M6.)

M11. Midpoint of an annual three-day walk (August 6-9) by Missouri and Kansas peace activists from the Bendix factory in Kansas City, manufacturer of plastic and electronic parts for nuclear warheads, to Whiteman Air Force Base, Knob Noster, Missouri, headquarters for Missouri missile deployment.

N5. On November 12, 1984, four Catholic peace activists broke through the gate, damaged the silo lid and other fixtures with a pneumatic jackhammer, crowbar, and smaller hammers, poured blood, unfurled a banner, and celebrated Holy Communion. After their arrest, trial, and conviction on sabotage and other charges, Federal Judge D. Brook Bartlett imposed these sentences: Helen Dery Woodson and Fr. Carl Kabat, 18 years; Fr. Paul Kabat, ten years, and Larry Cloud Morgan, eight years. In 1987 Paul Kabat and Larry Cloud Morgan were released on probation.

N11. On February 19, 1985, Martin Holladay spent 15 minutes inside the silo enclosure. He tied up a cloth banner reading "Swords into Plowshares," spray-painted "No More Hiroshimas," poured blood, and chipped the concrete lid and some electrical outlets with a three-pound hammer. His action was in support of four other peace activists who went to trial that day for damaging silo N5. Holladay was convicted of sabotage and other charges and sentenced to eight years in prison. On September 24, 1986, he was released on probation.

Chapter IV:
In Missile Silo Country

Editor's Note: The mapping of the Strategic Air Command's 1,000 Minuteman and MX missile silos and 100 launch control centers in 1985-87 was done largely by volunteers. Working in small teams, scores of women and men took to the highways and back roads of the missile silo states to produce the raw data for a series of six Nukewatch "citizen's action guides" to the missile fields of the Midwest and Great Plains. Inevitably, errors occurred.

To correct the errors in the maps and accompanying directions, Nukewatch decided to have each location double-checked. It was a formidable assignment. To accomplish it, we approached a Minnesota couple, Barb Katt and John LaForge, whose work for peace and justice has taken many forms over the last decade, including several jail and prison terms for nonviolent anti-war demonstrations. The two set out in early December, 1987, on an odyssey of 30,000 miles and 125 days. Staying at the homes of fellow peace activists, they put a geographic fix on each installation in the seven missile silo states and kept a journal. Here is their report. Photos are by the authors.

by Barb Katt and John LaForge

Tower City, North Dakota, December 8, 1987

FOG OBSCURED the outlines of our first missile silo. The sun never really rose, the sky just got a little lighter. We laughed to see the launch site emerge slowly from the retreating mist. But what was funny? We walked around the fenced enclosure, leaving our footprints in the snow and mud, peering through the wires at the humming thing inside.

One sign on the fence said simply, "No Smoking." Another read, "M24"—the Air Force's official designation for the missile and its nuclear payload, one of ten fired by underground cable from a launch control center about 25 miles away. A third sign appeared on

The authors.

all four sides of the facility. Its bold red letters warned us that this was a Restricted Area, that it was unlawful to enter without permission of the Installation Commander, and that while on the installation all personnel and their property were subject to search. "Use of Deadly Force Authorized." We were left to wonder what purpose warranted such a warning.

Before leaving, in a practice that was to become a ritual for us, we burned a sprig of sage, an herb traditionally employed to cleanse and purify. The dashboard of our second-hand Ford Escort was our altar. Covered with red cloth, it would come to hold stones, feathers, pine cones, bones, and other mementos of our four-month exploration of the thousand intercontinental ballistic missile silos of the Strategic Air Command.

We pulled up to silo D38 as our car radio was broadcasting news of the signing of the Intermediate Nuclear Forces treaty. The pomp and ceremony in Washington contrasted ironically with the grim and unadorned reality that surrounded us that day in the missile fields of the "Peace Garden State."

We were beginning to notice subtle differences in the poles, gauges, and other machinery that gird the massive concrete lid of an underground missile silo. Most prominent of these are the electronic sensors designed to alert security guards to the presence of intruders. At some silos the sensors are drum-shaped, looking like tubas, or ship-board ventilators, facing each other across the silo lid to form a magnetic field which, when broken, trips an alarm in the distant launch control center. Sensors at some other silos are metal triangles bolted at various heights to poles stuck in the ground. The sensor at D38 was a tall white pole with a conical tip.

Protruding from the base of each silo lid are two steel rails to guide the 120-ton cover clear of the silo shaft for maintenance work or when an explosive charge is fired prior to launching. Circular hatches in the concrete superstructure give access to the silo chamber and an adjacent utility room containing an air-conditioning unit set to keep the underground temperature a constant 69 degrees Fahrenheit. The low hum of the air-conditioner makes it sound like the rocket itself, anchored five stories below ground, is ready to take off. Surrounding each launch site is an eight-foot chain-link fence, topped with three strands of barbed wire, enclosing a graveled plot just large enough to let a helicopter land within. The gate is chained and padlocked.

We rattled the gate of D38 and left some sage to purify the ground. It was one of 28 silos and three launch control centers we had seen on our first day.

Union, North Dakota, December 13

The sun had set, and it was too dark to find more silos. So we set our minds to looking for "C0" (Charlie Zero), one of the 15 launch control centers, each controlling ten missiles, in the 150-missile Grand Forks Air Force Base complex. Launch control centers are built to blend into the countryside. Above ground, they could pass at first glance for ranch style houses whose owners are partial to chain-link fences, elaborate radio towers, and plenty of outdoor lighting. But, close up, there is no mistaking their military purpose.

Over the next few months we would encounter many a launch control crew, shoveling snow, playing basketball, or looking at us looking at them through binoculars. A crew of seven works a three-day shift at each control center. Pistols on their hips, the commander and deputy commander occupy seats at a con-

What purpose could warrant such a message?

sole in a concrete bunker deep underground, ready to turn keys that can launch nuclear war on 31 seconds' notice. Recently the Air Force, in a change of policy, announced that women would be allowed to join men in the performance of this fateful function. Should we draw comfort from this step toward women's equality?

Peter and Lorraine Holcomb, peace activists whom we were to meet later in Cheyenne, Wyoming, attend church with the commander of a launch control facility. "If the order came, I don't think he'd launch them," Peter told us.

We decided to verify the location of Charlie Zero that night. As we approached the likely area, we saw Christmas lights in the windows of a well-lit building in the distance. Drawing closer, we found the object of our search. The bunker that might some day launch the ultimate war this night was decorated for the Prince of Peace.

Merry Christmas!

Mount Carmel, North Dakota, December 14

Here, just a few miles from the Canadian border, we met the U.S. Air Force. First we encountered two armored cars—what the Strategic Air Command calls "Peacekeeper vehicles." The flat-sided cars—not much bigger than pickups—are painted olive drab. The occupants peer through narrow slits. Large, bug-eyed headlights glare, even in the brightest weather. A heavy, perforated, V-shaped bumper juts out in front of the grill, like a battering ram. The rubber tires are solid, rather than inflated, so the enemy can't shoot them out. On top is a round hatch cover that opens behind a flip-up shield notched for a rifle. More menacing than a Brinks truck, less imposing than a Sherman tank, these odd hybrids look incongruous at the Dairy Queens and on the back roads of rural North Dakota.

The two armored trucks guarded the highway about a fifth of a mile from our destination—missile silo B20. Two others blocked the gravel access road near the silo gate. On the silo itself, a flurry of activity was taking place around a large, white semi-trailer. Designated officially as a "Minuteman Payload Transporter," such vehicles look much like other 18-wheelers except for the bold, diagonal black stripes on the rear doors. The trailer is fitted with hinged panels which cover the silo lid when the vehicle is parked directly above it. With the concrete lid rolled out of the way, crews inside the trailer then have free access to the missile's nose cone and thermonuclear payload. We could see that the trap door under this trailer was wide open.

It quickly dawned on us what was happening at B20. Our fears tinged with exhilaration, we realized that we were witnessing forbidden secrets. How should we approach the armed guards? Should we approach them at all? Driving slowly, we stopped in front of the young men in camouflage uniforms, long enough to snap a photo.

A guard approached our car. He was friendly. Barb offered him a silo map and explained our project. Then we heard another guard say, "Call the marshal."

We decided it was time to leave. But before going John asked a question: "Changing the old warhead, eh?" The tight-lipped guard just smiled, and so John continued: "Oh, classified information. I understand." Then we drove off.

Even after dozens of such meetings, neither of us could overcome the fear and revulsion that accompanied our encounters with the Air Force's payload transporters—on busy highways, on the streets of small towns, and sometimes poised above the tip of a Minuteman missile.

If the Air Force sometimes made *us* nervous, the op-

posite was also true. One day, near the town of Inkster, John approached the fence to get a closer look at the goings-on at missile silo G16. A guard asked, "What business do you have here?"

"I live here," John said, referring to the planet Earth.

From inside the silo fence the guard gripped his M-16 rifle and declared, "Not on this property, you don't."

Just then, two maintenance workers crawled out of the silo hatch. They looked like sky divers in their orange jump harnesses over one-piece suits. Seeing us, a second armed guard ran between two Air Force trucks, calling to the workers and manipulating his hand radio. He seemed to be telling them to hide. We drove away, trying to imagine what it must be like to keep a nuclear missile in good working order. Sometimes we'd respond to such run-ins by giving appro-

Launch control centers could pass for ranch style houses.

priate names to the silos. Like "Stoking Ovens."

Dahlen, North Dakota, December 15

Our car had Minnesota license plates. You could tell from its coating of dust and dirt that it traveled back roads. Sometimes gas station attendants would ask us what we were doing out here. We would tell them we were checking missile silos—and we would show them our map. Occasionally we would remark on the hundreds of empty farm houses in this part of the country.

"You can't see the half of it," one attendant told us. "So many have been torn down you can't even imagine how many little farms there used to be out there. I drive a school bus, and I pass a lot of those silos. The roads with the missiles on them are a lot better maintained."

At the town of Dahlen, near launch site G20, we found little more than railroad tracks, a grain elevator, a few houses, and a row of shops that had been boarded up or left open and empty, their windows broken.

A friend, Barbara Mishler, now living in Minneapolis, used to spend summers in Dahlen, helping with chores and hanging around the elevator. She tells us she remembers watching the Air Force put in G20. A huge earth-mover drilled out the core. Tons of steel and concrete were brought in for reinforcement. Miles of wiring were laid, and finally a big truck with hydraulic lifts slid the missile into its hole—an open wound in the land she loved.

'You can't imagine how many farms there used to be out there.'

Mayview, Missouri, January 26, 1988

We came to recognize Air Force vehicles because they were generally similar from one silo field to the next, and we were by now familiar with their functions. Sighting a boxy green armored car—a "Peacekeeper vehicle"—told us that a payload transporter, carrying nuclear warheads to or from a silo, was not far away. Maintenance vehicles—invariably dark blue with gold lettering on the doors—ranged in size from pickups to bread trucks.

At silo N5, just off highway I-70 east of Kansas City, we encountered our first PMT—the "Periodic Maintenance Team" trailers with which the Air Force polishes its underground sabers. In Missouri, these semi-truck and trailer rigs were everywhere. What caught our attention was the garish insignia on these vehicles.

On the side of each trailer, facing forward, is the profile of an American Indian. His headdress is a white, three-stage rocket—a bonnet of feathered nuclear missiles. His mouth is open in a yell, or possibly a war whoop. Or could it be a cry of pain from the weight of this dreadful crown? We took pictures as the guards stood watching, feet set apart, rifle butts on their hips, barrels aimed skyward.

In Missouri and in other missile silo states we were often reminded of how the Native American legacy has been trampled in the name of Pentagon priorities.

In South Dakota, missile silos pock-mark the ancient Cherry Creek Trail, leading north from Rosebud, and the Deadwood Trail, leading into the Black Hills. Faded white signs point to these centuries-old Indian paths, now crossed and recrossed by gravel roads that lead to missile silos. Nearby, too, still visible, are the steep ruts cut in the prairie by the wagon wheels of white settlers.

Phillip McNally, a writer and teacher whom we met in Springfield, Missouri, has studied the American Indians of the Great Plains. He has traced the path taken by Chief Joseph and his band of 700 Nez Perces fleeing the U.S. cavalry in 1887, through what is now the missile silo field of Malmstrom Air Force Base in central Montana. Cornered by two armies, and with his people facing disease and starvation, Chief Joseph surrendered, saying, "I am tired; my heart is sick and sad. From where the sun now stands I will fight no more forever."

Will we some day have the wisdom to relinquish the engines of mass destruction we have buried in the ground and vow to "fight no more forever?"

Everett, Missouri, January 27

At missile silo L10 a young Air Force guard in camouflage suit and black beret ordered us to stop taking pictures. We ignored him, maneuvering instead for a better shot of the Minuteman payload transporter parked on the silo. Security guards clambered from their armored trucks, some shouldering automatic rifles. Walkie-talkies crackled. But no one attempted to interfere with us. They behaved, strangely, as though we weren't there.

We left shortly, thinking no more of what we'd seen. But within an hour a "Peacekeeper vehicle" was crowding our rearview mirror. It followed us from town to town and from silo to silo. Half a mile from L11 we found another payload transporter, swarming with security guards. The armored truck stayed on our tail for another 50 miles to a gas station in Harrisonville. While we pulled up to the pump, the truck crew parked across the lot, pretending to look the other way.

Barb walked over to where the two young men sat stone-faced, and signaled to them to open their window. The man on the passenger side slung a rifle over his shoulder and got out of the truck.

Nervously, Barb explained our project.

"Yes ma'am," was the only response.

Back at the car, we were joined by the young Air Force guard.

"Ma'am? You took some pictures of a sensitive operation this afternoon. Could we have the film from your camera?"

"No, I don't think so," Barb replied.

"We just want to see what it is you got on film, and we'll send back the negatives of everything that isn't restricted."

The Air Force had no legal grounds for confiscating our film, and we would not turn it over, so the young man asked for a missile silo map. Then he wanted our names, and some identification.

We gave him a map and our names, but refused to produce I.D. He seemed puzzled and hurt. Our conversations with the Air Force often followed that pattern: a series of their commands and our polite refusals.

The guards drove away before we had finished gassing up.

Florence, Missouri, January 29

Missile silo D10 is nestled among rolling hills covered with mixed hardwoods, mostly oak, and a few ancient pines that grew close to the silo fence. Across the road is a small abandoned house with a south-facing porch. We sat there, soaking up the sun and imagining what it would be like to live so near an ICBM.

Later that morning we met Ethmer Eriesmen, out chopping a hole through the pond ice so his cows could drink. Silo I10 stood humming across the road as we spoke with him across his barbed wire fence.

"I'm a member of the Church of the Brethren. That's an historic peace church. There's quite a large number of us here, and we have done sermons on these silos. I'm in favor of a strong defense, but these silos

They behaved as though we weren't there.

are way more than we need. I used to garden next to that silo, but I didn't like the herbicide they use on the silo so close to my food."

The land next to D4 near Tipton was strewn with farm machinery, some of it impeding the Air Force's access to the silo. The sight of such chaos in the presence of an ICBM was so unusual that we got out of the car to take pictures. We found the owner of the land working nearby, tending fruit trees.

"You must be selling something," said Earl Murphy as we approached. "The only people who would walk out this far in mud have got to be selling something." We shook hands and explained our interest in the silo on his land.

"Are we going to have a protest?" he asked, with a grin. "There's no way to beat the Air Force, I know."

Murphy told us of how he took possession of the land in 1986 and began planting an orchard of several thousand trees. Soon the Air Force told him it wouldn't allow trees to be planted close by—"snipers could hide in them." He was also told he would have to move his irrigation pond—snipers again. Several times he was required to uproot fruit trees planted over cables leading to the silo. but after much anguish he and the Air Force had come to an uneasy truce which allowed the trees and pond to stay.

Then came a legal order forbidding him to put up a building in a place he had leveled and landscaped. But Murphy maintained he'd received verbal permission from the Air Force to build. The case went to court, testing an Air Force rule disallowing structures within 1,200 feet of a Minuteman silo. (Land owned by the Air Force extends only 25 feet out from the silo fence. The purpose of the 1,200-foot rule is to protect the Air Force from liability claims arising out of damage or injury from the fiery exhaust of a Minuteman missile in the event of a launch).

Murphy lost the case.

Collins, Missouri, January 31

Lola Boswell of Collins is a retired attorney who has lived for 17 years with her two cats down a mile-long road on her family's 151-year-old, 297-acre homestead. She insisted on driving into town to pick us up because the creek had flooded over her bridge.

From the minute we met our overnight hostess, Lola engaged us in eager conversation of current events, and pressed us for details of our work against nuclear weapons. When Barb mentioned that for most of the summer we had been in prison camp for civil disobedience at air force bases, Lola exclaimed: "Good!

Occasionally we would leave documents, bones, and other souvenirs.

What did you learn in jail?"

"Oh, I've been in the fray," Lola said, forcefully. She had run for office once. "And boy did I learn all about me then. They said I had come to Collins to overthrow the government. Remember, you're in the Bible belt here. If you go against the government for any reason, then you're called a Communist."

At 78, Lola is still passionate and enthusiastic about politics. "Reagan is the most evil president we've ever had," she said with conviction. "Worse than Nixon."

Kansas City, Missouri, February 3

This afternoon we drove out to N11, near Odessa, Missouri, with Ursula and Martin Braun, two young West German volunteers at Shalom House, a Catholic Worker House in Kansas City, Kansas. They had never seen a missile silo. After we had walked around the installation, Ursula remarked in astonishment: "This is it? No guards? No dogs? In Germany it wouldn't remain undamaged for long."

We tied the silo gate shut with yarn, and wove a peace sign into the fence, as if to say, "We know what happens here." It had become our custom to do such things at missile silos. Occasionally we would leave weavings or pictures of our friends, sometimes with documents citing international law, sometimes bones, always sage, and, whenever possible, lots of cow pies tossed over the fence.

Dupree, South Dakota, February 24

We liked to share hot coffee from the Thermos and read the morning paper to each other during the long cold drives to the first missile. In South Dakota we read that state and federal officials were haggling over a couple of hundred million dollars to be paid to the Sioux Nation for what the Supreme Court ruled was the illegal confiscation of the Black Hills. (The Minuteman missile system has cost over 13 billion dollars to date).

The *Lakota Times* reported that nine of the 24 poorest counties in the United States are in South Dakota. The single poorest, with a per capita income of $3,244, is Shannon County, just south of a cluster of Minuteman silos. Dwight Call, regional director of the YMCA in Dupree, called the article to our attention during our three-day stay in his one-bedroom house on the Cheyenne River Indian Reservation. Dupree is a small town with dirt roads, lots of pot-holes, and a segregation all too common in the West: Indian people on one side of town, whites on the other.

Missile silos now dot the land of the Cheyennes. Dwight told us the legend of the "Woman Who Lives With Wolves." A woman was once separated from her tribe at the onset of winter, the story goes, and was close to death when she awoke to find a wolf licking her face. The wolf led her to a cave in a high craggy butte overlooking what is now missile silo F8. The animal brought her food until spring, when she was able to rejoin her people. Her descendants still carry the name, "Lives with Wolves."

We asked ourselves how our descendants would remember us.

Rapid City, South Dakota, February 27

We visited 24 missile silos this day, all silhouetted by the Black Hills on the distant southern horizon.

Half a mile west of launch control center L1 we came upon an unsettling assortment of high tech equipment painted stark white. A large sign read, "United States Air Force. Combat Evaluation." A smaller sign said, "Warning: Radio Frequency Radiation Hazard. Radiation in this area may exceed hazard limitations and special precautions are required."

Trailers with two huge rotating satellite dishes were parked near five trailers sprouting oddly shaped antennae. Cables snaked their way across the ground, connecting the trailers to a long barrel, looking somewhat like a cannon, pointed skyward. A dome covered part of the installation. We drove away wondering what sort of diabolical space age weaponry we'd found.

We learned from Marvin Kammerer, who ranches at the end of the Ellsworth Air Force Base runway, that the equipment was for monitoring practice bombing missions. The lights of the base shine through Kammerer's windows at night, and the windows rattle as the bombers circle. Kammerer, a "rancher for peace," has long opposed the military presence in South Dakota. At the end of the Ellsworth runway he and other activists have created three huge symbols from painted rocks, clearly visible to Air Force pilots as they land. The giant art works are an Indian medicine wheel, an ecology symbol, and a peace sign.

Bismarck, North Dakota, March 2

At a Presbyterian church here we heard a message from Father George Zebelka, spiritual adviser to Catholic crew members of the plane that bombed Hiroshima. It was a message that seemed appropriate for today's missile fields. He said:

> We must stop making war respectable. We've made it not only respectable but an honorable Christian profession: glorious, wonderful, and profitable. Now we must break through this respectability.

The glory and respectability of war are widely reflected in the missile silo country.

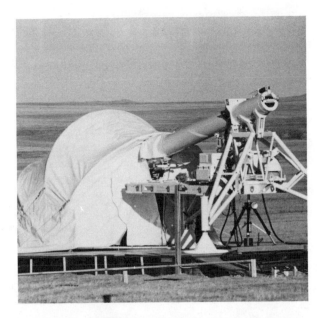

Space age weaponry on the South Dakota prairie.

In Kimball, Nebraska, which proudly calls itself "Missile Center U.S.A.," we found the town's tallest structure, high above a canopy of trees as you enter from the east, to be a kleig-lit Titan I ICBM standing boldly in the city park.

Missiles are displayed proudly in most of the missile silo fields. They are prominently featured at the Strategic Air Command museum in Bellevue, Nebraska, on the road approaching SAC headquarters at Offutt Air Force Base, where a stained glass window in the chapel depicts a tumultuous scene: the President's red telephone, Air Force bombers, a mushroom cloud, and an adoring pilot calling out, as in the Bible, "Send me Lord."

When we took the "Missile Drive" exit from I-25 in Cheyenne, Wyoming, we found ourselves approaching F.E. Warren Air Force Base, the "Home of the Mighty Ninety and the Peacekeeper ICBM," where three gleaming white rockets stand like sentinels at the main gate.

The main gate at Grand Forks Air Force Base in North Dakota displays a well-polished Minuteman missile and a row of retired aircraft. An entrance sign welcomes visitors to the home of the "Warriors of the North." (At Offutt Air Force Base the welcome sign proclaims SAC's motto: "Peace is our Profession".)

(The "Warriors of the North" were part of this year's observance of the birthday of the Rev. Martin Luther King, Jr., sponsored by the Black Student Union of the University of North Dakota at Grand Forks. Black airmen and officers from the base played a prominent part in the public tribute to this steadfast advocate of Gandhian nonviolence).

Not to be outdone by Kimball, Lewistown, Montana has erected a Minuteman missile in its city park. At Great Falls, Montana, local townspeople flocked this year to the "Sports-Auto-Rama" at Malmstrom Air Force Base, and "Friends and Neighbors Day" at the Grand Forks base. On such occasions the Pentagon customarily entertains guests with acrobatic stunts by its precision pilots, the Air Force's Thunder Birds and

Postcard from the Big Sky country.

the Navy's Blue Angels.

Makoti, North Dakota, March 4

Today, while driving over North Dakota's flat, wind-swept farm land—broken only occasionally by embattled windbreaks as straight as chalk lines—we stopped to look at a cemetery. Amidst the tombstones and artificial flowers and stiff brown grass, a white crucifix rose above a stone alter. At the foot of the cross stood the figures of Mary and John and two angels. Behind these timeless monuments, piercing the late winter sky, we saw a familiar configuration of poles behind a chain-link fence. It was Minuteman launch site F11.

Minot, North Dakota, March 5

We got to Ron Staff's house after dark. Ron greeted us like a brother. Over cups of hot herbal tea we shared stories about our work—ours as missile silo chroniclers, his as a counselor at the veterans center. Two worlds seemed to merge in his compact living room over the next four nights—his painful and often discouraging struggle to help ease the mental stress from past wars, our sobering research to prevent a future one.

Ron showed us a speech he had given at a Memorial Day service: "... we must be conscious of the dead our wars make, in order to imprint our conscience. When our conscience has been firmly imprinted... perhaps warring will be reined in."

Mohall, North Dakota, March 9

The stench of natural gas filled the air and oil rigs were everywhere on our way to missile silo 05, also known as "Oil Can Harry." A payload transporter and two support vehicles were on top of the silo, so we stopped to take pictures. An airwoman in camouflage gear slung a rifle over her shoulder and trotted to the gate to check us out.

"Come here," she commanded. We waved and left.

As luck would have it, our return route took us past 05 again about half an hour later. Evidently we were noticed from a long way off. The guards on the silo took defensive positions, kneeling with their rifles, while a security team awaited us at the access road. We drove past with a friendly wave while the security vehicle fell in behind us, beginning a pursuit that lasted the rest of the day and into the evening.

Everywhere we went, the Air Force went, too, even waiting outside a restaurant while we ordered pizza. The security truck followed us that night to the American Legion hall in the town of Mohall, where we attended an Air Force hearing on missile silo underground cable-splicing operations scheduled for that area.

Leaving the meeting momentarily to retrieve something from our car, we caught the Air Force's Keystone cops shining a flashlight in the front seat. Could they have been examining our dashboard horde of bones and stones and feathers? Seeing us return unexpectedly, they backed up hurriedly, turned around, and disappeared into the night.

Conrad, Montana, March 16

A huge, warehouse-sized structure three stories high loomed for miles in the rangeland north of Great Falls, Montana. A dozen squared pillars, part of an unfinished fourth story, rose above the flat-roofed building. The concrete and steel walls were three feet thick. The big metal doors had been removed, leaving the building to the pigeons.

We had come upon the remains of an Anti-Ballistic Missile site, abandoned in the 1970s even before it was completed. We poked through the small concrete rooms lining one wall, examining the shelves and bunks and other fixtures that never had been put to use. Someone had painted a human shadow on the wall and scrawled this message: "A 272 million dollar monument to America's stupidity."

Three months earlier we had visited an even bigger abandoned ABM site near Nekoma, North Dakota. It looked like an Aztec ruin: a four-sided pyramid rising above the flat fields, with a dark circular device on each side near the apex. Concrete towers of various sizes stood next to the pyramid. A compound of houses and warehouses the size of a small town stood boarded up nearby.

The images evoked by these monuments to death and waste were dissolved that evening by the vigorous expressions of life that greeted us when we arrived at the home of Gloria and Zane Zell and their five children near Shelby. The Zell family farms the land surrounding missile silo P1.

As an adolescent, Zane had not wanted his parents to sell the land to the Air Force for a missile silo. When the engineers arrived to prepare the land for silo construction, he had pulled up the survey stakes.

The protests at P1 have continued over the years. On this year's spring equinox we gathered there with 30 people—as many children as adults. A banner on the silo fence proclaimed, "Papa-1 is a noxious weed." We walked around the silo, shaking the chains on the

Silo J6: A view from the playground.

gate, leaving drawings made by the children, burning sage, giving vent to our healthy anger.

Hughesville, Montana, March 23

A golden eagle perched on a fence post near the first silo of the day. Hundreds of golden and bald eagles had been migrating through this area, feeding on gophers. We often saw deer and antelope grazing placidly near the silo fence.

We drove down a long, beautiful canyon carved by Maiden Creek. The warmth of the smooth cliff faces and the fresh scent of the pine trees left us unprepared for the sterile superstructure of missile silo A5, the ICBM we found buried in the valley floor. We had heard the silo was haunted by the spirit of an Indian woman who makes herself visible to Air Force personnel. It wasn't hard to believe.

The plateaus were semi-arid, and where a plow had broken the sod the topsoil was blowing away—great drifts of it—into the ditches. Clouds of dust blotted out the sun.

We found a rural elementary school in session just a thousand yards from missile silo J6, where a work crew was transferring nuclear warheads from a payload transporter as casually as though they were sacks of potatoes. The nonchalant security team let us take all the pictures we wanted and then advised us helpfully to call the Air Force public relations office for more information.

Later that day, in the center of Great Falls, a Minuteman payload transporter and four armored escort vehicles cruised past on the main street. "It happens every day," our hosts told us.

Roy, Montana, March 26

At the Bohemian Corners cafe, where the walls of the entryway are covered with auction notices, a waitress poured our coffee and asked, "What are you kids doing around here?"

We explained, and she pointed out her home on our map.

"They've been working on this silo for a week," she said, pointing to another place on the map. "I drive by there every day."

"How do people here feel about living around all these silos?" John asked.

"They love 'em," the waitress replied. "Brings in jobs."

Peetz, Colorado, April 1

A tall, thin man came out of the church to greet us. "I'm Ed Bigler. Welcome to Peetz."

Peetz is a High Plains farm town so small that it no longer supports a grocery store. But it does have two churches and a post office. For six years, every Good Friday, Ed Bigler, a Methodist minister, has led a group of parishioners and others to missile silo J3, next to the highway a mile and a half south of town.

This Good Friday we walked with him and about 50 others past the grain elevator and up to the fence of J3. We huddled in a circle and broke bread.

Several months earlier, at a smaller vigil at silo F6 near Warsaw, Missouri, a man dressed in coveralls, moved by the solemnity of the occasion, had spoken

'We're guarding that missile back there.'

up: "I went into Hiroshima a few weeks after the bomb was dropped. We used to take bets on whether the bodies floating past us on the river were men's or women's. Most of the time they were so badly burned and bloated that you couldn't really tell."

Now, in Colorado for Easter, we camped overnight next to J8, a force many times more powerful than the bomb that destroyed Hiroshima. About a dozen attended a sunrise service at J8 on Easter morning, with Ed Bigler presiding. In 24 hours of well advertised activity at the fence of this nuclear missile silo, no security patrol had put out from the launch control center, just a few miles down the road. (Perhaps we owe this uninterrupted reflective time to Mr. Bigler's consistent Easter witness).

Kimball, Nebraska, April 5

Near the Titan missile monument that dominates the city park in this western Nebraska community, we came upon a bored crew lounging around an armored Peacekeeper vehicle. John asked them if they found

Good Friday in Colorado: After the service.

the duty interesting.

"Yea, sure," came the sarcastic reply. "We're guarding that missile back there." Everyone laughed.

An airman complained about having to spend three days at a time in a metal box, referring to the armored car.

"It's a piece of shit," said another.

A third guard looked up from the raunchy magazine he was reading and motioned to the Peacekeeper vehicle: "They take a one-ton frame and put a five-ton body on it. No wonder the thing breaks up in a couple of months."

Taking note of this, we named the next silo, "Money Is No Object."

Harrisburg, Nebraska, April 6

We got an ice cold, stone-faced reception from the driver of an Air Force maintenance truck, with five guards aboard, who discovered us parked near the gate of missile silo F5. He almost blocked our exit. While John backed our car up in preparation for a getaway, Barb approached the Air Force truck, trying to be friendly. Then we heard the radio operator ask, "Should we call this in?"

"Let's go," John exclaimed, loud enough for all to hear. Since we'd parked within the Air Force's 25-foot "clear zone" skirting the silo fence, we were concerned about being arrested, as others have been for getting too close to missile silos. We drove away a bit unnerved, wondering if the marshals would soon be on our tail.

Eight silos and several hours later, we stopped for a nap in a small meadow under a rugged yellow butte. John clapped his hands to hear the echo—and a golden eagle swooped down on us and disappeared behind the butte. Just then an Air Force truck stopped behind our car and an officer, with binoculars facing in our direction, cried out, "There they are!"

Our hearts sank. But, while pondering the terms of surrender, we realized that the attention of the two men had been focused not on us but on two golden eagle nests built into the cliffs just above us.

We laughed at ourselves, then climbed up to explore the nests. The rock crags and shelves surrounding the nests were littered with the remains of many an eagle meal: gopher and rabbit bones, skulls, femurs, spinal columns, jaws, feet, pelvises. Feeling like grave robbers, we left with enough skeleta to mark silo F6 with a skull and cross-bones.

Brownson, Nebraska, April 7

Like a town dug by giant prairie dogs, the huge, earth-covered mounds marched row on row to the horizon, covering ten square miles or more. Signs warning ominously of contaminated water and polluted soil meant nothing to the cows that grazed contentedly among the bunkers.

Looking for missile silos of the High Plains, we had come upon an abandoned World War II munitions factory. The Sioux Ordnance Depot, once a major employer in this area, was declared surplus after the Korean War. The federal government sold the land and buildings to the State of Nebraska, which reopened the depot as Western Nebraska Technical College, now Western Nebraska Community College. The only military presence still remaining is a small, fenced-in compound in a remote corner of the campus—the site of launch control center G1.

We swung open the heavy steel doors of a bunker and looked in on great piles of cool, sweet-smelling wheat—an odd contrast with the fading, 40-year-old safety notices still posted on the door. Opening the door of another bunker, we found it empty. We stepped inside, our footsteps echoing against the walls. A mouse ran toward us, drawn by the light of the doorway. We shivered as the ghosts of war rolled out on a wave of cold air.

You could tell which silos were being converted to MX.

Little Horse Creek, Wyoming, April 8

Last on our list of missile silos to check were the 50 in Wyoming—Flights P, Q, R, S, and T—where the Boeing Corporation, under contract to the Air Force, has been replacing Minuteman with MX. The MX is a four-stage rocket that carries ten precision-guided nuclear warheads, each independently targeted. The Pentagon describes it as "an advanced, high-throw-weight MIRVed ICBM."

The profusion of trailers and construction gear clustered around silos in this area told us which ones still were in the process of being converted to MX. We found cranes, trucks, trailers, buses, vans, and bulldozers assembled for the building of a deadly new missile system.

From the Wyoming hills, graders have carved broad new highways for giant tractor-trailers to deliver the 70-foot rockets to their fortresses. These majestic avenues, freshly striped and studded with brightly shining reflectors at each curve, end abruptly at the silo gates.

At one such site we slipped into a port-a-potty and left a sticker with crossed Soviet and American flags. It read, "Peace on Earth."

Herrick Creek, Wyoming, April 9

At silo P3 we could tell something important was happening. Four armored trucks and two U.S. marshals guarded three bulky work trucks and two payload transporters. We arrived at the fence to find one of the bomb trucks lowering the trap doors that fit over the silo. We got out of our car and took pictures.

The two marshals drove out immediately and parked behind our "Farms not Arms" bumper sticker. As some of the workers waved merrily to us from the silo enclosure, a marshal got out, "just to call in the license number." He asked if we were tourists.

"Well, there's no law against taking pictures," he said, and then returned to the silo as an armored truck drove out to block the access road.

Its access road freshly graveled, utility pole refurbished, launch tube broadened and lengthened, and its generator humming, P3 and its deadly plutonium warheads were loaded. MX would soon be ready for launch.

As we stood for a moment, staring, an Air Force guard poked his head out of a window and yelled, cheerily, "Isn't it pretty?"

We shouted back, "Not really!"

A Family Outing

Editor's note: What is it like to spend the night next to a nuclear missile silo? One person who has done so is Tom Fox, editor of the National Catholic Reporter in Kansas City, Missouri. He and his family camped out at missile silo D9 on the night of November 9, 1985, as part of a weekend vigil by peace activists at many missile silos in the Show Me State. Here is his report, reprinted by permission of the National Catholic Reporter, P.O. Box 419281, Kansas City, Missouri 64141.

by Tom Fox

IT WAS NEARING dusk when we arrived at our designated missile site on Highway 52 just a few miles west of the small town of Stover, Missouri. Some friends, Tom and Margaret Montgomery, who had not yet driven to their own site, had accompanied us for moral support. We pulled our trusty 1976 Volare station wagon onto a gravel road and immediately came to a gate upon which was a sign: "Keep gate closed." Uncertain of what we were getting into, we opened the fence gate and quickly carried in our tent and sleeping bags. Within minutes, we had set up camp.

Darkness was all too quickly upon us. The Montgomerys, after brief hugs and promises of prayers, were off. And now we sat—my wife, our three children, myself and our dog.

We brought along two flashlights, and one had already begun to fade. As we sat there in the dark (we wanted to save our lights in case we had to leave in the middle of the night), it seemed time to explain to ourselves what in God's name we were doing, sitting there in a farmer's field in a tent, feeling quite exposed, at the outset of what we knew would be a chilly November night. A few hundred feet away was a Minuteman missile tipped with a warhead containing the explosive force of 1.2 million tons of TNT. It hummed during the night.

"We are here," I remember saying, "to choose between gods, to choose between the worship of weapons and the worship of a loving, protecting, merciful God." We broke bread, shared it and prayed for courage.

The children were trusting enough. My concern was not the Air Force security patrols or local sheriffs. They could kick us off the site if they chose. Inconvenient as that might be in the middle of the night, my real concern was local folks who might decide they wanted to make a statement of their own—at our expense.

Also going through my mind was a more personal note. How would we manage to keep the peace within our very own tent? In such proximity, a wayward elbow at any moment might spark an outbreak of violence all of its own. This might be a very long Saturday night.

"Daddy, what time is it?" Catherine, seven, would ask

Huntley, Wyoming, April 10

No one was present at silo S4 when we arrived on a Sunday afternoon. We were amazed. Of almost a thousand nuclear missile silos we'd seen in four months, this was the first one we'd found with the lid open. We thought of throwing something into the hole, to undo the preparations for MX, but an Air Force helicopter whirred overhead, and we let the thought pass.

The open silo lid was one of many anomalies we encountered in missile silo country. On the door of an MX construction trailer at a silo soon to house this monstrous new weapon, we noticed a sign that said, "Danger—Microwave Oven in Use." Amidst unimaginable destructive power, the illusion of normality is tightly held. We remembered the words of a school bus driver pleased with the smoothness of the roads near the missile silos, of the waitress thankful for the new jobs, of a journalism teacher who remarked to us, off-handedly, "Well, if anything happens, at least I'm toast."

Who is responsible for the thing that could happen? The waitress? The teacher? The Air Force crews who tend the instruments of destruction? We ourselves?

With every silo we left humming, every missile we left undisturbed, we had to acknowledge our own complicity.

Deer Creek, Wyoming, April 11

T3. The last silo. We shut off the car motor and for a minute just sat there staring. Then we gathered the things off the dashboard and took some food to go sit by the missile.

We laid out the red cloth and arranged the pieces picked up on our 30,000-mile journey, reminding ourselves of when and where we had found each one. A jack knife from a hitch hiker in Montana, a hand-made doll from a friend in Kansas City, pine cones from the Black Hills, bones and feathers from the eagle's nest, a dozen other trinkets. We lit some sage and sat a long while in silence.

Then we brought out lunch. Our mood lightened, and we celebrated. We had a long way to go still. Tomorrow we were due in Omaha for a court appearance for friends and for another demonstration at the nearby headquarters of the Strategic Air Command—nerve center for the missile fields. With any luck we would be there in time.

with unnerving frequency. Odd, time seemingly had never been of such concern to her before.

Then around eight in the evening, we had our first visitor. A car drove up and parked outside the fence. A man got out and began to shine a flashlight on our tent. It was a local sheriff's deputy.

I came out and asked whether he had been informed in advance of our protest. All state law enforcement agencies were supposed to have been notified. He said he had heard nothing. "Well, let me tell you why we are here," I said, seizing the opportunity to address our skeptical visitor.

"You are trespassing on private property."

"We arrived at dusk, and there was no one in the area to ask," I replied respectfully.

"You are still trespassing. If I get a complaint, you have to leave."

"Agreed. But let me tell you why we are here. There are 150 missiles buried underground in the area, and on each is a weapon capable of destroying a city the size of Kansas City."

"You've got to be kidding. A hundred and fifty? Why here? Why not in Kansas City?"

"Because the people here are good and decent and are not known to oppose their government's decisions. And the air base puts money into the local economy."

"Are they dangerous?"

"If one would go off, it would level everything within, say, 10 to 15 miles," I replied.

The deputy said the Air Force had told local residents 20 years back that in case of an accident, only an area up to 300 yards around the missile would be within the danger zone.

About 25 minutes later, our conversation ended with the deputy thanking me for our action, saying he would contact his congressperson to register a complaint. He also noted he was overwhelmed by the map we produced. He asked for a copy to share with his friends.

During the night, Air Force security patrols came by several times, but only asked questions once, and that was after some early morning light had made us more visible. They were always polite but a bit cold.

Our children have long known their parents get involved in unusual activities. But that night in the farmer's field is one they are unlikely to forget for some time. I hope one day they recall it in light of the first commandment.

Driving away from the site, my wife, Kim Hoa, summed up our feelings. "I feel very good," she said. "I was afraid and overcame my fear."

We all agreed it comes down to where you finally place your trust.

Chapter V:
Beacons of Hope

THE DAWN OF THE NUCLEAR AGE in 1945 marked the birth of a worldwide movement—strong in the United States, as elsewhere—to put the genie back in the bottle through international control of atomic energy and atomic weapons. It was a nuclear weapons prevention movement led, fervently, by scientists who had designed and built the first atomic bomb, then recoiled in horror at the casualness with which it was put to use as an instrument of national power politics. But the move to have the Bomb turned over to a supranational authority foundered on the shoals of the early Cold War, leaving "ban the bomb" efforts to a dwindling remnant of concerned citizens.

The cause of nuclear disarmament lost its mass base in the anti-Communist and anti-Soviet hysteria of the 1950s. But what hurt the movement even more was a strategic shift on the part of its leadership, particularly liberals, scientists, and academics. The shift was from rejection to acceptance of nuclear weapons—a resigned, regretful acceptance, but acceptance nonetheless—rooted in a sense of *real politik*. For many people concerned about nuclear weapons and the danger of nuclear war, the question became how to control the arms race, not how to stop it. An "arms control" community—anchored in academia, in the Democratic Party, and ultimately in government itself—came to power in the Kennedy-Johnson era. It has continued to frame nuclear weapons issues through every succeeding presidency.

The first major achievement for arms control was the Partial Test Ban Treaty negotiated by Kennedy and Khrushchev in 1963 under intense worldwide pressure to curb radioactive fallout from nuclear weapons testing in the atmosphere. The treaty placed restraints on one phase of the U.S.-Soviet nuclear competition, requiring nuclear weapons tests to be conducted underground. In doing so, it enabled the testing to continue unchallenged. Next came the Nuclear Non-Proliferation Treaty of 1968, in which the nuclear weapons "have" nations (five at that time) effectively narrowed the field by offering nuclear power technology to the "have-nots" in exchange for their commitment not to develop atomic arms of their own. Next, the Anti-Ballistic Missile (ABM) Treaty of 1972, in which the superpowers mutually agreed to refrain from developing an unworkable and expensive weapon concept that each independently was ready to shelve. The ABM Treaty marked the start of a series of Strategic Arms Limitations Treaties (SALT-I in 1972, and SALT-II in 1979—the latter signed but never ratified) in which the United States and the Soviet Union placed comfortably high ceilings on various long-range delivery systems and agreed on mutually verifiable force strengths. SALT-I set the maximum number of U.S. fixed-site missile silos at the pre-planned level of 1,054. But it allowed the nuclear arms buildup to continue unrestrained through the MIRVing of the U.S. strategic system— that is, substituting new missiles with multiple warheads. The next advance for arms control, after a pause to accommodate a Reagan Administration buildup, was a mutually agreed upon decision to withdraw intermediate-range nuclear forces from Europe, but without constraints on redeployment of the displaced warheads. In each case—from the Partial Test Ban Treaty of 1963 through the INF Treaty of 1988— the politically powerful nuclear weapons establishment has exacted a price for its consent. The price has been permission to "modernize" the nuclear weapon systems along lines of its choosing. As their price for agreeing to SALT-I, for example, the U.S. Joint Chiefs of Staff secured Nixon Administration support for accelerated development of the Navy's Trident submarine and the Air Force's mobile missile. Each new arms control agreement has spawned or accelerated new weapon systems, some of them justified as "bargaining chips" for the next round of arms control negotiations. In this way, arms control has helped open the door for new nuclear weapons systems that came to be well entrenched: the B1 bomber, the cruise missile, multiple warheads on strategic missiles.

In accepting these terms (however reluctantly), the arms control community has become the collaborator of the nuclear weapons establishment. The history of arms control essentially has been a history of power sharing between the weapons establishment and its loyal opposition. Little wonder that arms control advocates are to be found not just in universities and liberal think tanks but in the offices of military contractors, in nuclear weapons laboratories, and in the Pentagon itself.

With the signing of the INF Treaty in Moscow, in June 1988, attention turned to the next arms control step, a Strategic Arms Reduction Treaty (START), initially proposed by the Reagan Administration and later enthusiastically embraced by the new Soviet premier, Mikhail S. Gorbachev, as a way of relieving the military burden on the hard-pressed Soviet economy. Initial START negotiations looked toward reductions of 30 to 50 per cent in the strategic missile forces of the two sides. Like the Partial Test Ban, ABM, SALT, and INF treaties, START commands wide support because it appears to bring restraint, stability, control, even diminution, to the nuclear arms race. But an agreement limited to a single category of weapons can have only the opposite effect. It would simply redirect the momentum of the nuclear weapons buildup, as have other arms control agreements, into new paths.

There are additional reasons why the military is prepared to bargain away its fixed-base intercontinental ballistic missiles. Developments in missile guidance technology (led by the United States and followed by the Soviet Union) are rapidly rendering long-range missiles obsolete. The time is approaching when each side will be able to hit the missile silos of the other with pinpoint accuracy, greatly conserving the number of warheads available for other targets. Furthermore, Minuteman also is becoming physically decrepit. The computers still may hum sweetly deep inside the launch tubes, but in a quarter of a century the elements have taken a heavy toll on the steel and concrete of the underground casings. In the mid-1980s the Air Force spent half a billion dollars just to repair the corroded electrical pumping systems to keep the silos from filling up with water. Within the next few decades Minuteman is almost certain to crumble away, a victim of remorseless natural forces. The weapon system may already be on its last legs as a "credible deterrent." Nature is in the process of disarming Minuteman.

WITH THE RETIREMENT of Minuteman in sight, what vehicle will carry the fortunes of the Strategic Air Command and the rest of Minuteman's vast constituency into the Twenty-First Century? Already waiting are two competing mobile missile systems (one on rails, the other on wheels) and, just over the horizon, a galaxy of space-based weapons now fetuses in the womb of Star Wars laboratories. If past experience is a guide, the transition to the new weapons will be presented as a necessary "modernization," touted as a step toward peace, and loyally accepted by the arms control community.

But Minuteman's impending departure also presents an extraordinary opportunity for the American public to deal comprehensively with the nuclear problem—

so dangerous to the world and so destructive of the economic and social fabric. The question of whether and how to replace a major element in our apparatus of strategic nuclear deterrence will arise at a time of unparalleled change in that other nuclear superpower, the Soviet Union, which is the supposed object of nuclear deterrence. At bottom, the selling of a new weapons system, like the selling of the arms race itself, has always depended on the selling of the Soviet threat. The growing openness and democratization of Soviet society under Mikhail Gorbachev, coupled with the increasing economic burden of the arms race on the economies of both superpowers, makes the selling job more difficult, promising to dissipate the climate of militarism which perpetuates Cold War policies in the United States. The mellowing of U.S.-Soviet relations strikes at the heart of the nuclear deterrence rationale which sustains not only our intercontinental ballistic missiles but the entire edifice of nuclear arms.

There is another reason why the missile silos of the nuclear heartland will present an unusual opportunity for Americans to reverse historic national security policies in the 1990s. The reason stems from Minuteman's unique characteristic of being accessible to the public. No other nuclear warheads can be closely approached. No other nuclear weapon delivery system can be so readily seen, heard, touched, confronted. No other object presents the same opportunity for people, singly or in numbers, to get in touch with nuclear Armageddon—and with their own potential for dealing collectively with the common danger. The opportunity is a fleeting one. It will be gone when, with the departure of Minuteman, the palpable power now encased behind wire fences in open fields and prairies retreats into inaccessible recesses of remote military installations.

If we grasp the present opportunity for acknowledging and dealing with the common danger, then the missile silos of the United States are worth more to the doves of this country than to the hawks. The "gods of metal" would best be left in the ground as bargaining chips of our own for comprehensive measures halting or throttling down the nuclear arms race in all its aspects, such as a ban on *all* nuclear weapons testing. In the absence of real nuclear disarmament, these aging but still menacing missiles should continue to serve as tangible, visible, approachable evidence of a larger unseen danger. So long as they remain in place they will continue to present our best and last hope (short of the catastrophe of nuclear war itself) that the American people can be roused to deal with humanity's most urgent problem.

So far, it is only the faintest of hopes. Here and there, Americans have begun to acknowledge responsibility for the missiles. Some have gathered at the silo fences as a way of confronting policies that countenance the waging of nuclear war. A few have gone over or through the fences, raising confrontation to the level of resistance, often at great cost to themselves. The numbers are pathetically small. But they are growing. The smallness of the numbers does not adequately measure the degree of public concern about the nuclear danger. Rather, it reflects the invisibility of the missiles, still as hard to notice as the arms race itself, and the widespread perception that little can be done about the problem.

But, like the arms race itself, and more than any other single weapons system, Minuteman—alone in the fields and prairies—depends on a climate of public acceptance. It is more vulnerable to withdrawal of public consent than to incoming Soviet warheads. The numbers at the silo fences will swell, and the vulnerability of the system will grow, when Americans begin to acknowledge the missiles as their own, when seeing a missile silo comes to be thought of as part of seeing America, when going up to or even over the fence comes to be regarded as a civic duty akin to voting for President or joining the Air Force. The swelling of the numbers into the tens of thousands—no more than you'd find in many college football stadiums on an autumn afternoon in any of the missile silo states—would send a powerful signal through the land. The signal would say *no* to the cosmetics of arms control, *yes* to the substance of nuclear disarmament.

The missile silos of the nuclear heartland are beacons of hope. Given the will, we can fashion instruments of peace from the deadly warheads in our soil.

Wendy Weiss

MISSILE SILO SCULPTURE

Wendy Weiss, assistant professor in the Department of Textiles, Clothing and Design at the University of Nebraska, Lincoln, created this sculpture—"Prairie Missile Site: Silent Silo"—after participating in a South Dakota missile silo vigil in 1987. It was exhibited in the spring of 1988 at Nebraska Wesleyan University in Lincoln.

The idea for the sculpture developed out of a desire to convey to the public the eerie presence of the missile silos on the Great Plains. She used a weaving to represent the missile, choosing white plastic tubing both to define the shape of the missile and to allude to its invisible yet ever-present nature. The weaving—17 feet high and 7 1/2 feet across—was hung from a tree limb and surrounded by 20 tombstones cut from pine and engraved with excerpts from texts relating to nuclear missiles. On the backs of the tombstones she embedded brass bullet casings.

A sample text, taken from a transcript of a Senate Armed Services Committee hearing on a defense authorization bill:

SAC Commander in Chief, Offutt AFB, NE, Gen. John Chain: "[Deleted.] These forces provide the 'insurance policy' that allows us to deploy the 2nd 50 Peacekeepers in a manner that allows [deleted]."

They stand out like carbuncles, eerily silhouetted against the menacing grey banks of prairie clouds, an alien presence in a rich pastoral scene.

—Alex Brummer in *The Guardian,* London, October 1986.

Missile silo I40, near Lakota, North Dakota.   © **John Hooton**

For the Silo Pruning Hooks

by Helen Dery Woodson

Forgetful earth
by human treachery now damned
her creatures' modest need neglect
gives but a grudging portion for her children's fill
and in unfruitful labor thus
anticipates the sterile scape of death.
Her victims
sprung like rotting teeth from dragon's horny jaw
their eyes scratched senseless in the stony waste
seek answer from her barren breast.
And will you give a million tons of fire
instead of bread? How long
O Lord?
How long?
Where still unshattered sacred voices fly
where martyr's copious blood yet feeds
the fragrant soil
our hammers rang with urgent song.
May hardened steel be bent
in mercy's grasp
and concrete split beneath perduring truth.
May earth again redolent
pungent, sweet
revoke her mindless curse
and yielding to her Lord's unceasing love
let peace and justice sear her bleeding heart.

(Written in the Jackson County Jail,
Kansas City, Missouri, November 1984)